# LIGHT A FIRE UNDER YOUR BUSINESS

# LIGHT A FIRE UNDER YOUR BUSINESS

## How to Build a Class 1 Corporate Culture through Inspirational Leadership

Tom Pandola and James W. Bird

Foreword by G. H. Worth

PRAEGER™

An Imprint of ABC-CLIO, LLC

Santa Barbara, California • Denver, Colorado

**Library of Congress Cataloging-in-Publication Data**

Pandola, Tom.
    Light a fire under your business : how to build a class 1 corporate culture through inspirational leadership / Tom Pandola and James W. Bird ; foreword by G. H. Worth.
        pages cm
    Includes bibliographical references and index.
    ISBN 978-1-4408-3458-5 (print : alk. paper) — ISBN 978-1-4408-3459-2 (e-book)    1. Leadership. 2. Corporate culture.    3. Success in business.    4. Fire departments—Management.    5. Success in business.    I. Bird, James W.    II. Title.
    HD57.7.P357 2015
    658.4'092—dc23        2014044470

ISBN: 978-1-4408-3458-5
EISBN: 978-1-4408-3459-2

19  18  17  16  15    1  2  3  4  5

This book is also available on the World Wide Web as an eBook.
Visit www.abc-clio.com for details.

Praeger
An Imprint of ABC-CLIO, LLC

ABC-CLIO, LLC
130 Cremona Drive, P.O. Box 1911
Santa Barbara, California 93116-1911

This book is printed on acid-free paper ∞
Manufactured in the United States of America

# Contents

# Foreword

Many people such as you and I have attended numerous business management seminars or national conferences in our fields of industry and read books about the business world's "latest and greatest" breakthroughs for management excellence. These innovations supposedly illustrate the secrets for leading employees and developing successful leaders. However, many times the new and "hot" subjects for success are, truthfully, the same old basics that have been wrapped in the latest jargon or publicized in notable professional business publications in order to sell copies.

*Light a Fire under Your Business* is an exciting guide to better business practices. The authors are two former professional firefighting leaders who successfully transitioned to become professional business authorities in their respective industries. They offer real firefighting experiences that result in the saving of lives and protecting properties and show how these experiences are relevant to improving similar business practices with the goal of saving business lives and inspiring initiative in leaders and employees.

I met Jim Bird, a coauthor of this book, during my early years as a struggling entrepreneur. In such early days, as you surely already know, your business is built on hard work, long hours, and choosing the right people. Sometimes—more importantly, in critical times—the decisions regarding whom to recruit to assist in helping you overcome obstacles, rectify seemingly insurmountable difficulties, or take on a project of many unknowns that could be vital to your future existence really come down to a gut feeling. Jim fulfilled that role on a number of occasions over the years for our company, St. Ives Laboratories, Inc.

As my small company grew, I called on Jim, since I knew that he was a firefighter and that he had a varied work schedule, to complete several tasks important to the growth and expansion of our consumer-packaged-goods company. Money was tight, and I needed dependability, honesty, and confidence that any task or project I assigned would be completed satisfactorily. Over the years, there were many occasions, in several diverse disciplines, when St. Ives faced obstacles or projects critical to our business's growth that required special handling. We needed a person with no established St. Ives responsibilities to be able to focus on the assignment.

These projects, over several years initially, were taken on and managed by Jim on his off-duty days from the fire department. His work with us assisted in the rise of St. Ives Laboratories, Inc., to become a multi-million-dollar, international health and beauty care corporation.

Although I never worked directly with Tom Pandola, the other coauthor of this book, over the years, Jim has shared Tom's business world accomplishments with me. Following the end of his career with the Los Angeles City Fire Department, Tom's full-time duties included managing and administrating a fleet of rescue helicopters and emergency personnel for many years. It was explained to me that Tom's nontraditional business leadership practices, initially, were not acknowledged by his supervisors as anything special. Then, one day, a business consultant working for the company asked him what he was doing differently in his region. The consultant had noticed that those under his leadership had a more positive attitude, they demonstrated appreciation and respect for others, and major problems just didn't seem to occur. Tom simply said that he handled his region the same way he handled his battalion while serving as a fire battalion chief with the LAFD.

To the point, Tom had taken the initiative, within the scope of his responsibilities, to make changes by training his subordinate leaders to be more influential and inspirational. Jim emphasized to me that Tom's actions had created improvements that are supported by the principles in this book.

I am certain from the values, the assessments, and the experiences Tom and Jim share throughout their book that their suggestions, instructions, and advice will be insightful to any business management professional like you. They have taken their lives as firefighters—ultimately as fire captain and fire chief—and used the fire service management values and principles by which they survived and prospered in their professional firefighting endeavors and then excelled when they each adapted those same principles to their particular business world.

I know this for a fact, as I personally witnessed Jim's rise in our corporation and his successes internationally, which assisted in the sale of my St. Ives Corporation to a multi-billion-dollar international company. That corporation, Alberto Culver, a consumer-packaged-goods company, did not include a department in their organization similar to the department that Jim had built for me at St. Ives Laboratories.

In the transition of St. Ives Laboratories to its new ownership, the department that Jim built and managed on an international scale for St. Ives was put on the chopping block. It was to be eliminated, along with Jim.

My staff and I, including the corporate CFO, endorsed Jim's department, including its organizational uniqueness and operational successes. We were able to convince the Alberto Culver Company transition team that they should not eliminate the department but, rather, take advantage of its management qualities for their company.

Our advice was heeded, and the department remained intact. Additionally, Alberto Culver soon increased Jim's role with the St. Ives products to also include operations in the corporation. His new responsibilities included the addition of such products as Alberto VO5, Tresemme hair care products, NeXXus, Motions, and several other Alberto Culver brands.

Jim's successes ranged in the tens of millions of dollars annually, eventually exceeding nearly $200 million in total sales. This department that Jim designed and administrated, which in the Alberto Culver Company had previously never existed, also took them into a commerce channel in which it had never ventured. Impressively, the revenues realized were incremental to the company and, in fact, had never existed previously. In other words: It was new money.

More impressive were the events carried out by this new department and the methodology utilized to reduce costs through multi-interdepartmental management and leadership. The increases in profitability realized up to 300 percent increases annually at times. These achievements resulted in Jim's department receiving many corporate goal-breaking awards over many years and personal corporate recognition for Jim and his associates.

The business experiences and successes by Tom and Jim have been quite similar. Both transitioned from firefighting professionals to become successful business professionals without previous business college training or business experiences. They improved quality and efficiencies through unique management methodologies. They implemented improvements in training regimens, quality assurance procedures, and professional disciplines.

Both have attributed their business successes to their adaptations of the fire service management and leadership principles they each lived by for over 20 years. Both of these former fire officers accomplished these transitions and implemented their adaptations of the fire service principles and management procedures to their individual business operations. What is more astounding is that both have accomplished these transformations and successes in completely separate and unassociated industries.

There were times in our business when St. Ives's middle management and upper management executives would say, "I don't know how he's doing it, but Jim's department is exceeding all expectations." I'm certain Tom's history in business has had similar results with similar associates, or superiors scratching their heads the same way.

Many business professionals, possibly including you, have heard in their national, regional, or corporate meetings that the current state of affairs is in a life-and-death situation. They wonder, "How did we get here?" "What do we do now?" "How could this have been prevented?" The fire service principles, the quality assurance procedures to follow, and the leadership strategies and tactics presented in the pages of *Light A Fire under Your Business* can be successfully adapted to most business situations and can possibly prevent most of those times relating to situations that caused the similar previous three questions.

The advice given in these pages can provide an organized method to construct a comprehensive business culture that can instill pride, confidence, and professional determination in your company's leaders, personnel, and associates. The tools that Tom and Jim suggest can help give the leaders and personnel of your company excitement in their daily tasks. The visions that are conjured through the fire and rescue stories are related to business situations and can make a connection to unmistakably demonstrate how these approaches can instill urgency in leaders and business associates determined to succeed in their business endeavors.

The use of these various tools can produce a culture in a company that will not accept failure. Leaders and your associates will look at their jobs as being as important as those of firefighters, or fire officers, who cannot tolerate mistakes. This can inspire attitudes that must continually achieve improvement and that can be as rewarding as saving a life or saving a home.

Long hours, hard work, and choosing the right people have a lot to do with achieving success. But long hours, hard work, and choosing the right people can become monotonous, overly demanding, and personally exhausting. A company's most important and most expensive resource is its people. Giving your people some new, fun, and exciting methods to use to accomplish their goals can be rewarding for you as a business owner, senior executive, administrator, or department manager as you see them succeed.

The tool kit found in the pages of this book will be fun to use, with an added reward of improved effectiveness, and efficiencies!

G. H. Worth, Founder and CEO,
St. Ives Laboratories, Inc.

# Preface

The majority of the fire service accounts you will soon read are written by former Los Angeles City Fire Department Battalion Chief Tom Pandola. He and I share similar experiences in both firefighting and business, and we have teamed up to collaborate on developing the principles of business leadership and organizational culture explored throughout this book. We are former firefighters who became successful leaders in non-firefighting businesses. To be more specific, we are two ordinary people who served as fire officers upon whom a great deal of responsibility rested. During our fire service careers, both Pandola and I successfully worked many years in the rank of captain; he was promoted again, to the rank of battalion chief.

We first met midway through our fire service careers, when I was assigned under his command as a young engine company captain with the Los Angeles City Fire Department. His firefighting leadership reputation was well-known throughout our 3,000-plus-member metropolitan fire department, which served nearly four million citizens. I felt privileged to be under his command and anticipated significant professional growth opportunities.

During this period, prior to my departure from his command, I learned of his interest in business enterprises. He shared innovative ideas for several ventures, and we discussed what life would look like after our fire department careers came to an end.

We went on our separate ways for many years, and unbeknownst to one another, each of us was busy applying our experiences in firefighting leadership and emergency-management principles to become highly successful business team leaders. In separate and very different business organizations and occupations, we have been responsible for helping to improve strategic and tactical management for small and midsize companies as well as large Fortune 500 corporations. Our individual business-related work resulted in millions of dollars of incremental revenue for our employers. By following the same leadership style and using the same principles of operational effectiveness and efficiencies that we employed during our firefighting careers, we were able to create work environments that produced continuous improvements within our spheres of influence. The results were increased profits for our respective employers.

Many years later, I found myself working for a corporation based in Chicago. I had the opportunity to share business insights and past experiences with some of my supervisors and peers. Upon discovering that I had completed a 24-year career in firefighting and rescue work, some of them suggested that my problem-solving and decision-making abilities during stressful business situations must have had something to do with the firefighter in me.

It was then and there that it hit me: I had been using my previously learned, ingrained fire service management and leadership principles to guide me in my business profession. I compiled a list of successful business experiences to examine how and why I had consistently improved in my corporate career without any prior formal business education. I found that the culture I brought to my business career had made me so successful that my supervisors made me feel like a star performer.

In our fire service careers, we constantly needed to be prepared to respond at a moment's notice to an ever-wider variety of unknown and completely unique situations—preparation was the key. Additionally, careless mistakes in our procedures and actions could cost lives and was not tolerated. Maintaining a focus on success was mandatory. Continuous improvement was crucial.

Applying this fire service attitude—this culture—in my business career had paid off. My business successes were numerous and were recognized on several occasions by my superiors in two Fortune 500 companies.

I instinctively thought of my friend, former Battalion Chief Tom Pandola. I contacted him and discovered that he had been busy in his post–fire service life as well. He had previously spent a few years working in leadership development training and had moved on to be a very successful regional director and team leader in the emergency air medical transportation industry. We exchanged our similar business success stories—experiences we believed were due to adapting our firefighting principles to fit our new work situations.

We discussed our mutual ideas for developing business management and leadership principles that had originally been tested during our fire service careers. We became certain that we could help others to continuously improve businesses and create successes as we had done. We both declared our commitment to further develop and share our fire-tested and business-proven career experiences. If successful, we could be back in the business of helping others to continuously improve their management processes, empower their people through inspirational leadership, and transform the culture within their organizations in a positive way.

It is our vision that this book will provide our readers with the same proven principles for management, leadership, and success that have the power to continuously improve business operations, personnel motivation, and the bottom line.

Jim Bird

# Acknowledgments

We want to thank the following people for being a part of making this book possible.

Our families, your understanding and support are priceless;

Suzi Bird, for always going above and beyond to help out;

Dave Murray, for providing insight, encouragement, and friendship;

Laurie Stevens, an author and friend who reviewed our manuscript and gave us excellent advice;

Maryann Karinch, our agent for taking a chance and believing in our message;

Gary Worth, who enthusiastically contributed the Foreword;

Marshall Goldsmith, for graciously taking the time to read and endorse our book;

The Praeger Publishing editors: Hilary Claggett, Michelle Scott, Erin Ryan;

Pete Feely, for providing watchful oversight of the copyediting;

Kristiana Burtness, for copyediting our manuscript into a book;

Every one of our fire service and business colleagues for your friendship and notable examples that have shaped our way of thinking.

# Introduction

In 1736, Benjamin Franklin organized Philadelphia's Union Fire Company, the first fire department in that city. Knowing that an uncontrolled fire had the capacity to destroy an entire town—including everyone and everything in it—Franklin's efforts were a matter of survival. His famous and insightful saying, "An ounce of prevention is worth a pound of cure," was originally aimed at inspiring early firefighting and fire-prevention improvements.[i]

A lot has changed since the days wherein firefighters from Franklin's Union Fire Company were regularly seen racing through the streets of Philadelphia to extinguish dangerous fires. Yet, to this day, there is one thing about firefighting that has not changed. Firefighters have always had the need for continuous improvement to survive very dangerous and potentially deadly work environments. Because of this very important point about firefighting, one might say that this book is a story of survival. In some ways, it is.

The stories in this book are actual experiences from our combined fire service careers of nearly 50 years, plus our combined business careers of nearly 30 years. They are presented to you, the reader, to demonstrate a particular point or principle. To some readers, this book could seem to be about us or about the fire service; it is not. More accurately, we refer to our past experiences because our fire service careers acted as a practical classroom in which we learned the principles that have served us well in firefighting, subsequently in business, and in life in general.

Have you ever desired to be the best at what you do? If so, this book is for you. It's also for those facing challenges every day in their work or personal lives, where all the signs appear to be telling them to give in or give up. But they don't. Or perhaps once they did quit and failed, but now truly desire to finally succeed. This book is for them.

This book is for all those who feel that something is missing in their work. More specifically, it relates to how they feel about what they do and why they do it. It is for those who are looking for a feeling of importance in their workday and, ultimately, their work life. You will learn in the following pages that in the fire service, this feeling becomes a way of life; it is what we call a Class 1 Culture.

Knowing the risks and being vigilant is a matter of life or death for firefighters and their leaders. Isn't the same true for the life of any organization, business professional, and those who lead in the business world? If the most recent financial meltdown, involving things from failing banks and auto recalls to government regulators—who were apparently asleep at the switch—taught us anything, it is that something is missing. Along the road to success, some businesses seem to have misplaced their view of what they do and why they do it. Had business and government incorporated some of the leadership and cultural principles of the fire service, perhaps their leadership teams would not have been caught off guard, as they appear to have been.

Surviving and producing success in firefighting is essentially about being continuously aware of the situation and, when necessary, being prepared to respond in extraordinary ways. Principles in firefighting compel leaders to inspire their followers to think of success and not even consider failure as an option.

When businesses fail—over and over again—many times it is an indication that people at multiple levels have lost their situational awareness. Part of the reason this occurs is that people forget, or maybe never knew, the importance of what they do and why they do it. How to do the work isn't the issue. The "how" is usually what businesses and organizations know and do best. Therefore, the "how" isn't the problem that typically causes strategic failure; we believe it is the "what" and the "why" that can cause organizations to lose their focus. It is mandatory to have a firm commitment and belief that what you do is important and that why you do it to the best of your ability is because it always matters to someone. Without such a commitment and belief, people can easily stray off course and lose their focus.

Firefighters succeed because, from day one, they believe that what they do is so important that they become motivated to be the best. Why they believe this is rooted in a culture that exists throughout the fire service. To develop such a culture is where leadership makes an enormous difference. Firefighters live with a resolve that success is mandatory, and failure is not an option. It takes inspirational leadership for such an organizational culture to exist.

We hope that you will enjoy the stories from the challenging and dangerous world of firefighting, but keep in mind that the goal is not to turn anyone into a firefighter. Our goal here is to demonstrate how these principles have already been adapted to create business successes. The principles that work to make firefighters successful will work for any individual or group of people. These same principles have already been proven to be highly relevant and effective in creating extraordinary successes in several types of businesses and organizations.

If you are like most people, you care about doing the best you can, no matter in which task, occupation, profession, or position you find yourself. Sometimes people just need a new attitude to, once again, believe in themselves. People make up the cultural fabric that exists within a company or organization. We can weave a positive, success-driven culture or unravel into a negative culture whose motto is, "Who cares?"

We believe that the vast majority of people have a desire to make a difference and want to do the right things for the right reasons. It can be difficult to see why our actions matter in some professions, tasks, or jobs. Feeling a sense of gratification from the fruits of one's labor can sometimes be difficult for people. You might even find yourself thinking that there are no opportunities for heroics in your job. Maybe you are working in a profession that was never your dream, yet there you are, unhappily working away, convinced that your work has little meaning and isn't worthy of your best efforts. If any of these examples describe your thoughts, please keep on reading. The fact is that all jobs are not created equally, and organizational leadership and culture aren't utopian. That is precisely the reason this book was written and why you should read on to see how anyone can do better in work and in life with a different perspective.

In the following pages, we share with the rest of the working world what we believe makes firefighters continuously focused on success. And success belongs to anyone who believes it's possible, who knows how to define it, and who is motivated to create it.

## Note

1.  "A Quick Biography of Ben Franklin," http://www.ushistory.org/FRANKLIN/info/, accessed July 30, 2014.

## Part One

# Improve Your Process

This first part of the book focuses on how to improve your process, something that is heavily dependent upon leadership and organizational culture. The first three chapters will cover where our adapted principles have come from and fire service experiences that illustrate the topic of process improvement, including workforce and leadership development, strategic thinking, and continuous incremental improvement in search of best practices. Through the use of fire-tested and business-proven principles of management, leadership, and success, we share unique ways to improve your organization's process.

When problems arise in any organization, the causes are usually either a process issue or a people issue. However, the fire service puts a great deal of energy into providing a process that supports the best efforts of those who serve.

- In chapter 1, we explore the process necessary to develop a motivated and inspired workforce.
- In chapter 2, we share a strategic thought process that improves decision making and can turn anyone into an accountable and empowered problem solver.
- In chapter 3, we explore the benefits of a process that delivers continuous incremental improvements as well as the discovery of best practices for you and your organization.

# 1

# Ordinary People Responding to Extraordinary Situations

*A leader is one who sees more than others see, who sees farther than others see, and who sees before others do.*

—Leroy Eims

It was good to be out of that basement, yet at the same time, I had an unbelievable desire to go back in and do it all over again. I had overcome a fearful experience, extremely grateful for the way that things turned out; I couldn't help thinking back on that moment when I lost sight of my dream.

I was kneeling in the doorway and looking down into the darkness that led to the basement stairwell. I knew only one thing: I wanted to quit. Being engulfed in the heat of the heavy black, suffocating smoke belching up from below made me reassess a long-held personal desire. It had been my dream to be a firefighter since I was 13 years old. Now, I found myself in the Los Angeles City Fire Department's academy, seconds away from going down into a dark, hot, smoky abyss, and yet my mind was telling me that this had all been a big mistake.

It suddenly dawned on me that I didn't want to be a firefighter after all. I didn't know what was down there, and I was just a dumb 13-year-old kid when I hatched this silly dream. *No,* I thought, *this isn't for me, and I need to quit!*

Just as I was convincing myself that I needed a career change, standing up to tell the training captain that I had experienced a great epiphany and that I was wrong about wanting to be a firefighter, I heard one of the captains say in a thunderous voice, "Okay, get down there and go find your victim!" With that, I was suddenly and forcefully pushed from behind by the four other rookie firefighters as they all responded in unison to the captain's orders to enter the basement. I was forced down into total blackness—very much against my better judgment, I might add.

I stumbled down the flight of stairs, inhaling hot gag-inducing smoke. Once at the bottom, I experienced absolute darkness. Before I could even think about what to do next, I heard a familiar voice shout, "Go ahead and hook up to your air supply!" It was one of the training captains down in the basement; somehow, even with the obvious hindrance to sight, he was watching over us. I felt thankful for his presence, as it made me realize that this was possibly going to be okay.

The captains had wanted us rookies to get a taste of smoke. This was to ensure that we would experience just how awful smoke really is to a living organism's ability to survive. It also served to demonstrate to each recruit just how important the self-contained breathing apparatus (SCBA) is and how it made survival possible, allowing firefighters to work in poisonous atmospheres.

On the captain's command, I quickly hooked the loose end of the air hose that dangled from the face mask—which was fitted snugly to my face—to the regulator of my SCBA. I began breathing the fresh air from the metal cylinder attached to a harness on my back. The cool air poured into my lungs as I started to find composure. I decided that as long as I was still alive and somewhere down there, one of our captains was watching out for us, I might as well start looking for the victim. On this training night, the victim was a bag of sawdust.

I began to focus on and rely on what I had been taught and had practiced for days before. Staying low to protect myself from the extreme heat banking down from the ceiling, I was on my hands and knees, following the wall with my right hand while searching with my left hand. In a sweeping motion, I moved my gloved left hand back and forth, sliding it along the floor, hoping to find the victim.

It was so dark in that basement that my eyes were nearly useless. I could hear the captain's voice in my head from an earlier lecture, wherein he said, "It is so dark inside a burning building that you have to learn to see with your hands." I kept repeating in my head, *See with your hands . . . see with your hands.*

I found myself acting as the leader of this group of rookies, and it brought a whole new meaning to the old saying, "the blind leading the blind." As I crawled around a corner, I could actually see something through the thick blackness. I made out the faint, eerie glow of the fire that was producing all of the heat and smoke. As I continued my search, I thought about how strange it seemed that such a small fire could produce so much smoke and heat. I also came to the realization and appreciation for the fact that the smoke was our biggest obstacle to achieving our goal.

Suddenly, my searching hand hit something. I quickly felt it with both hands . . . Eureka! I found it! It was the victim, a bag of sawdust. I had never been so excited to find anything in my life. My adrenaline was flowing, and my heart felt like it was going to pound itself out of my chest.

Together with the other rookies, I reversed course. Now, just as we had been trained to do, we were each feeling the wall with our left hand and making our way through the darkness back to the stairwell, carrying that bag of sawdust to the safety of the great outdoors.

I was so glad to be out of that basement, and I immediately removed my protective clothing and equipment, having sweated profusely under its weight.[1] The total weight of this gear added an additional 50 to 60 pounds for each of us to carry, which made for an exhausting search-and-rescue experience. Even with the physical challenge that the added weight caused, we all appreciated the benefits that every piece of gear provided, especially the SCBA, in protecting us from the intense smoke and heat.

Yes, it was good to be out of that basement. But I couldn't get over my unbelievable desire to do it all over again. I didn't know it at the time, but this entire experience was a small part of a much larger element of organizational culture that focused on the basic understandings of how extremely important and, usually, dangerous things are done. This well-developed plan from the leadership of the fire service was focused on ensuring that every rookie not only learned the skills of firefighting but also learned the culture that made it all possible.

My comfort zone had been stretched, and there was no turning back. I was grateful that I had gone the distance and that my long-desired firefighting career had been launched.

## Comfort Zones—The Bigger the Better

Everyone has comfort zones, and some are larger than others. Our comfort zones are where we live within our thoughts. They are how our mind tells us what is safe and comfortable as it represents our personal reality of what we believe is possible for us to do.

To expand our comfort zone, we need to do something new—something we haven't experienced before. This creates another experience that is no longer unknown to us and no longer seems uncomfortable. To truly stretch our comfort zones, we need to have an experience that scares us. Not something reckless that doesn't have any purpose other than to frighten us, but something that we really don't want to do and should do.

When people face their fears, their thoughts are no longer locked within the boundaries that they tend to build for themselves. This can allow self-confidence to soar as people emerge from their own basement experience, whatever and wherever that may be. Following my basement experience, with my confidence soaring, I felt like I was a firefighter. And I couldn't wait for the next opportunity to prove it.

After a brief period of time, all five of the rookies in my group, including me, discussed our shared experience. I found that the other recruits had experienced feelings very similar to those I had faced. We all agreed that in our prior lives, if someone had told us to go where the air was deadly, the heat was extreme, and we weren't able to see where we were going, we would have surely turned down the offer. The common sense that we had developed up to that point in our lives told us that it was crazy to go into the basement. And yet, for some reason, we did it anyway. At that moment, we were all looking forward to the next time.

Still, this all seemed unusual to me. Only 20 minutes earlier, I was ready and willing to throw away my lifelong dream if it meant I didn't have to go into that basement. Now, I was not only on my way to becoming a fire-fighter but also embarking on a journey of self-discovery. It wasn't yet clear how this would occur, but I would discover a lot about myself in the weeks to come. I was an ordinary person suddenly put on a path to respond to extraordinary situations. Thanks to a process that I wasn't yet aware of, I was about to witness how it worked, up close and personal. This process was all about preparing ordinary people for extraordinary situations. And it would eventually change me, along with every one of my peers.

## Ordinary to Extraordinary

There have always been many productive uses of fire. Unfortunately, when fire is allowed to escape these uses, we have unleashed one of the most powerful and destructive forces of nature. Firefighters are our communities' first line of defense against this destructive and potentially deadly foe. Firefight-ers, quite simply, are men and women doing a job. Many people think of firefighters as brave and heroic, but how do they become that way? How do ordinary people become firefighters who so confidently respond in the face of awesome dangers, while also making life-or-death decisions as part of their day-to-day routine?

Through this experience with the expansion of my personal comfort zone, along with the validation by my peers, I discovered that when new firefighter recruits arrive, the first day at the fire academy, many of them have the same fears as anyone else. They are afraid of fire, heights, and blood and guts, especially their own. As we all agreed, we were also afraid to fail.

Doesn't this describe most people? Think of a time when you arrived for the first day at a new job, a new promotion, or a new class at school; perhaps you were handed a project or task that you had never done before. These situations and many others like them can provoke significant stress and fear for most of us.

So what was it that made you stick with it, even while you were probably experiencing the fear that accompanies those great unknowns in our lives? Or maybe you didn't go the distance. What was it that made you quit? What might have given you the strength to stick with it and succeed?

A major factor that compels us to attempt accomplishing something is desire. It's the initial desire to achieve something that leads us to action. As a 13-year-old boy, I didn't know much about what a firefighter did, but I had the desire to become one because what little I knew looked pretty cool to me. That initial desire never left me, and it became my goal in life to fulfill this childhood dream.

Flash forward nine years, and as I looked down into that hot, dark, and smoky basement, which was new territory for me, I discovered that desire alone would not prepare me to respond to this extraordinary situation. I had also discovered the truth about achievement: Ordinary effort isn't good enough for achieving the truly important things that we want out of life. Successful people must develop and prepare themselves, throughout their lives, to progress from ordinary to extraordinary.

The fire academy cadre is accountable for the safety and development of ordinary people. It is responsible for teaching the recruit how to do the work that is the duty of the fire service. This includes ensuring that each rookie becomes skilled in performing that duty in the hot, dirty, and dangerous environment that defines firefighting. Each individual must learn, become proficient, and develop confidence with new skills. The focus of these skills is to prevent him or her from falling prey to the noise, distractions, and competing priorities that are so prevalent in firefighting and rescue situations.

## Erasing Real and Understandable Fear

This chapter is dedicated to revealing a process ordinary people must experience to believe that they can be extraordinary when the opportunity presents itself. If this developmental process can work for the fire service to erase many human fears and inspire extraordinary responses in the presence of fear, just think what it will do for you, your team, and your entire organization.

Rosalyn Carter said, "A leader takes people where they want to go. A great leader takes people where they don't necessarily want to go, but ought to be."[2] Generally, we can trust in someone to take us where we ought to go if we believe he or she has our best interest at heart. Bona fide, trustworthy leadership requires responsibility to those who follow. By definition, trust is a firm belief in the reliability, truth, ability, or strength of someone or something. It is one in which confidence is placed.

It is important here to remember that, just like my first experience in the art of firefighting, the new firefighter recruit does not by nature want to go into a burning building. The reason ordinary people run out of burning buildings is due to a real and understandable fear. This is the same fear many rookie firefighters bring with them into the fire academy.

The desire to become something they're not will only get the recruit into the fire academy. It's that person's "ticket to the dance." What it takes is excellent leadership built on trust to persuade new rookies to charge courageously into those burning buildings. They must overcome their initial fear, because this is how the job is done. They must be inspired to do it well. It is what they must do to save lives and protect property. It is what they will do throughout their professional fire service career.

There is a mental toughness that will develop within each of us if we have trusted influential leaders to convince us that something is possible. Modern-day philosopher, author, and world-renowned speaker Jim Rohn has said, "Managers help people see themselves as they are. Leaders help people to see themselves better than they are."[3]

By Rohn's definition, the fire academy captains demonstrate why they are some of the most successful leaders known. The proof is in their abilities to take ordinary people and prepare them both physically and mentally to see themselves better than they are at that moment. They do this, in part, by providing the inspiration for these people to successfully and enthusiastically respond to extraordinary situations.

Firefighters all over the world run into burning buildings while others are running out. They perform death-defying rescues, ranging from those at great physical heights to those down in raging, rain-swollen rivers and storm channels. They respond to every type of emergency known to humankind and, sometimes, even to animals.

As in the fire service, in business, people are the common denominator who will deliver either success or failure. Those who have the desire to follow a certain career path will also have the capacity to grow and develop when guided and inspired by capable, influential, and trusted leadership.

Trusted business leaders will be able to expand comfort zones by building self-confidence within their trainees, or apprentices. Trusted leaders provide encouragement with watchful oversight. They manage, direct, and lead in a similar fashion to the training captains who provided me with reassurance and reinforcement in that basement.

The fire academy captains are officers entrusted with the time-honored responsibility to create firefighters out of ordinary men and women who come from all walks of life. Because of the efforts of the training captains, every rookie succeeded that night in the basement, responding to the assigned task in the presence of fear.

These training officers are former firefighter training recruits themselves. Now fire-tested professionals, they are selected due to their experience and fire service accomplishments. They are trained with the skills necessary to pass along their knowledge to perpetuate the culture that places enormous value on becoming, and ultimately being, the best. Throughout their careers, they have led firefighters into physically and mentally challenging situations and know from firsthand experience what the profession of firefighting and rescue work demands. As leaders, they inspire through example, by showing the new firefighter recruits how to master every task and skill necessary to not only serve as firefighters but also to survive as firefighters.

The rookies learn to trust these officers with their lives. They learn that they must, as each day brings a new fear to overcome. The leader's knowledge and experience is what teaches the how-to. But for each rookie, self-confidence and courage flourish in an environment that also allows for opportunities to overcome their fear of the unknown. This process coincides with the rookies developing trust in their leaders. Much of this growth and progress is accomplished through their daily academy comfort-zone expansion experiences, along with the watchful guidance and encouragement from the captains.

Without trusting in our captains, none of the rookies in my academy class or I could have experienced the emotional growth of going into a basement fire. It wasn't something we had ever done, and because we were ordinary people with the same fears as most, we wouldn't have gone into that basement if we didn't trust the captains more than we feared the unknown.

If you're in a position to lead, please keep this thought in mind: Leadership can come from anyone. It can be found anywhere, from the CEO of a major corporation to the receptionist at the front door or someone in a club, on a team, or within a family. Leaders are not defined by position or pay scale. True leaders can exist everywhere two or more people assemble together. Leadership positions are best served by those who believe that they have a responsibility to those who follow them.

Think of an individual who is dealing with a challenging or fearful situation. You can be that person's mentor or coach if you are seen as a trusted leader who, in the darkest times, is there to show the way. It takes trusted leadership to develop the self-confidence and courage in others, allowing them to overcome challenges as they climb to the next level of performance—helping them to become better than they think they are.

## Up and Over

The fire academy is much like an amusement park that is home to attractions that are the basis of fear for the new firefighter recruits. However, unlike an actual amusement park, where most everything that produces fear is an illusion, the challenges that provoke fear in the academy are real.

When things don't go as planned, people can get hurt, and people can die. This is precisely comparable to the real world for which this "park" prepares rookie firefighters. One of the "attractions" at the fire academy is a six-story concrete building that looks quite ominous. It can be seen from blocks away by the rookies as they drive to the fire academy for the first time and every subsequent day they are in training. It is a little bit like the Matterhorn Mountain at Disneyland because it is an awe-inspiring, distinctive landmark. It's not as pretty, yet inspires suspicion and curiosity amongst the inexperienced academy rookies.

It was built with the ability to burn fires within it, over and over again. The six-story building is stained with black soot from years of countless training fires. It is equipped with exterior fire escapes on one side, and on the opposite side is an iron ladder bolted to the exterior wall that extends vertically from the first floor all the way to the roof. I remember wondering, *Why is that ladder there? It's possibly some sort of maintenance ladder*, I reasoned.

This building is referred to as the "drill tower," because that is what it is. It allows firefighters to drill on their skills in realistic environments encountered in every metropolitan city across the country. The fire academy experience for the rookies in the LAFD is actually referred to as "the tower." In fact, this is the site where most of the fear is generated for new rookies, with the belching of smoke and flame, the scaling of its height, and many more seemingly insurmountable challenges, such as the drill tower's basement.

Having the ability to train in real-life settings is as important for firefighters as it is for someone in any profession. Obviously, you wouldn't want your airline pilot to have only read about flying a jetliner prior to taking off with you and your family aboard. Industrial technology teams would not enjoy a very high success rate if they had never actually trained on computer hardware and software applications prior to being tasked to determine why your network went down and how to fix it.

The drill tower is used for training and evaluating each rookie's performance for a majority of the procedures and skills he or she will need when responding to the first actual fire emergency as a member of a fire company.[4] This includes: hoisting hose lines aloft, rescue-rope rappelling, extinguishing fires, ventilating smoke, raising and climbing ladders, and many more critical tasks.

One of the more memorable days in the fire academy is when rookies discover the purpose for that iron ladder bolted to the side of the six-story drill tower. Their discovery all starts with the captain's verbal command, "Up and over!" And that's what we did.

It was a cool autumn morning the first time I heard one of our captains say those unfamiliar words. I looked up the side of the drill tower and noticed there were other captains in the window openings at floors number three and five and a captain on the roof. As I watched the line of rookies ahead of me making their way up the iron ladder, I could hear the captains shouting encouraging words like, "Come on—you can do it! Did you think *all* fires were going to be in one-story buildings? Let's go, let's go! Hand-over-hand, let's go! You're not tired!" Of course, the point of these reassuring words was to keep things moving while keeping everyone's mind on the task, not on the danger.

When it was my turn, I realized that the higher I climbed (we were expected to "run" up the ladder), the tighter I gripped the rungs with my gloved hands. Just as I had been taught to do, I climbed that ladder with my eyes focused on the center of the next higher rung. Staying focused, I alternated my grip on the center of each successively higher rung—from my right hand to my left hand; my legs simultaneously propelled me upward.

As this quick repetition moved me higher and higher up the side of the building, the stress I felt was making the cool autumn air feel like a sauna. I realized that if I slipped or lost my grip, I was going to die!

In the same way that my conventional wisdom had told me that going down into a hot smoky basement was crazy, I was not feeling very good about this up-and-over thing either. I guess it's true that not everyone is afraid of heights, but I do believe that everyone is afraid to fall from heights. This was going to take strength, not only physical but also inner strength to trust in myself to hang on as I climbed all the way to the roof. Our leaders were there to assure our safety and success. But it was focusing on over-coming my fear of failing that helped me to find my inner strength and to conquer my initial fear of falling.

## If They Can Do It, So Can I

There is an inner strength we call self-confidence or courage. There is another level of strength that came to me from the group dynamic. I felt that I shared a common purpose or mission with all firefighters, especially my fellow rookies, and that gave me strength to overcome fear of any kind. I felt that if they can do it, so can I.

I didn't want to let my captains down. I also wanted to prove I was wor-thy to serve alongside my peers. This group dynamic transformed into true teamwork. The feeling of trust that I had for my leaders was followed by a feeling of respect for both my leaders and my peers. And I didn't want to fail in front of people I respected. Soon we were performing this climb two or three times per day. Before long, the up-and-over drill was as much second nature for the entire class as putting on our uniforms. Again, our comfort zones had been expanded.

Firefighters must continuously improve to survive very dangerous and potentially deadly work environments. Firefighters, we were learning, live by a set of principles that allows them to be effective at saving lives and protecting property. The reason that this type of training is necessary is that right now, not far from where you are reading these words, there is a team of firefighters prepared and ready to answer your call for help. Depending on where you live, some are paid professionals and some are volunteers, and they are all providing your community with a better quality of life. When the bad things happen, who are you going to call? Most of the time, it's going to be 911. And within minutes, firefighters will arrive at your location, ready, willing, and able to do their best to solve your problem.

What did it take to physically go up and over the drill tower to train rookie firefighters to perform a necessary but dangerous skill? The same ingredients needed to go up and over any obstacle in your organization. There was oversight and encouragement from trusted leaders, a focused approach, the opportunity to develop courage, a common purpose within the group, and respect for others.

The knowledge and ability to do anything is built on previous accomplishments by others. The captains provided the opportunities—new experiences for the rookies—every day to develop new skills. The academy captains had earned their right to present these challenges by way of experiencing their own firefighting and rescue successes and failures.

Every rookie performance, skill, and procedure was evaluated to be certain each of us understood what we did right and what we did wrong. The captains would continuously set expectations for incremental improvements in each of us. On a daily basis, they drilled the knowledge and skills into us that we needed to improve and strengthen to demonstrate that we were proficient.

Working, practicing, and planning to respond for success within a group that shared a common purpose was developing confidence within each of us and in each other. The captains understood that the process for creating the emerging teamwork was important to follow to instill these principles into each of the rookies. This is because teamwork is the basis for all fire service operations and is critical in assuring success in extraordinary situations.

Even failure feels different to those in a group or team when the group did its collective best, but that just wasn't good enough. The affected group recovers from a failed effort more quickly for the same reasons individuals feel a sense of energy and power from the successes of the group. Feeling the support from our teammates, and providing our own dedication in supporting each of them, amplifies the triumphs and softens the agony of collective failure.

Firefighting is a team effort. Firefighters, we were taught, are team members that go the distance because they always go together. This is a cultural element of firefighting. Companies and organizations of all types and sizes should embrace this very important cultural component. This type of teamwork will move your business team's performance from ordinary expectations to extraordinary efforts and accomplishments. How can you apply personal desire, trusted leadership, and teamwork to go up and over the obstacles encountered in your company, in your career, and in your life?

## Mission to Motivation

One of the first important concepts firefighter rookies learn in the Los Angeles fire academy is the mission statement: "To save lives and protect property."[5] Similar to most successful business mission statements, it is short and to the point. This characteristic assures that it is understood and will become the foundation for thought and appropriate action for every member of the organization. There is no room for misinterpretation.

The success of this mission statement can be verified by inspecting the actions of the members of the organization. This statement, we were told, is stated in priority order: lives first and then property. It doesn't matter whose life is being threatened—citizen, firefighter, even animals of every kind—all are included. It doesn't matter what is threatening the lives or the property—fires, floods, riots, earthquakes, or even killer bees—all hazards are included. The mission of the fire service is the duty upon which firefighters are sent.

When a fire chief arrives on the scene of a major emergency, such as a third-alarm fire with many people trapped, this shared mission statement will be the foundation that drives the decision-making process. The fire chief will develop and implement a plan that will save the most lives and then protect the most property possible.

Making my way through the fire academy, I was observing and experiencing how ordinary people face their fears. We were more successful because we were guided by influential leadership, as well as a belief in, and adherence to a mission statement that helped us to develop the self-confidence and courage to get the right things done for the right reasons.

### 🔥 Hot Tip

Your people can't believe in a foundational mission if it hasn't been defined by a well-written statement. They won't even think about it if it is too long, making it too difficult to remember.

If your company doesn't have a mission statement, create one. If you have a statement that is long and full of words with questionable meaning, making it difficult to remember or to interpret, improve it. Provide your teams with the underlying foundation upon which their every decision should be based. Begin to experience the benefits of having a focused organization with a well-written, concise mission statement.

It is easier to respond to extraordinary situations when we know, collectively, the expectations of a shared mission. The importance of a meaningful mission statement is that it provides for everyone within an organization the duty upon which they are sent. Understanding the mission builds self-confidence, which in turn creates the courage to be innovative to get the right things done for the right reasons, even in unfamiliar and difficult situations.

Courage isn't the absence of fear; it is action in the presence of fear. Self-confidence provides inner strength and the courage to respond even when we feel fear. Comfort zones are expanded when we overcome fear by replacing it with confidence built on experience, knowledge, and understanding.

When I completed the up-and-over challenge for the first time, I experienced an inner strength that came from the group dynamic. But it was our shared mission and the belief that I was part of that mission that helped me find the motivation to succeed. As a new convert to this omnipresent mission, I was also beginning to understand the vision of my leaders and how I was to contribute to that vision. I was now able to overcome fear with a greater emotion—inspiration.

As we were the newest members of the LAFD, our training captains knew that they needed to teach us about everything that related to this new world we had just joined. Every day they would set a powerful example—in both words and actions—about the importance of our foundational mission like on the day that one of the captains said, "The only stupid question is the one that doesn't get asked." This was a clear and understandable example to ensure that each rookie realized the power of clear communications and the dangers of miscommunications. This simple statement also set the tone for the expectation that there is no excuse for not being informed, an expectation that is a lifesaving part of the fire service culture.

A common mission also has the power to crowd out uncertainty within the group. Instead of your people being unsure of what to do, the certainty of this mission will be reflected within the group dynamic as it builds each individual's inner strength and confidence. Simultaneously, this serves to create the group expectations that build trust and confidence in each other. Embracing the mission statement is where teamwork is born.

Leaders at all levels must hold themselves and every leader in the chain of command accountable for demonstrating how thought and action starts with the mission. To be fully successful, it is mandatory to lead and support your people by encouraging them to think and to act in support of this common purpose. The right mission drives motivation.

## Share the Vision

Leadership for a group must provide the vision for a desired end result. To ensure that it becomes a reality, it must be remembered that a vision is a desired future state that must be shared continuously with all members of the team or organization. The more comprehensive the vision, the greater its effectiveness will be for all to see and to believe. Establishing the vision is only the first step in creating desired future outcomes.

A vision statement and a mission statement are very different from each other. A vision is a specific set of desired future accomplishments. Once achieved, a vision statement needs to be updated for a new and powerful future.

Remember, a mission statement provides a general guiding philosophy that gets to the core purpose of what it is that the group, company, or organization is in existence to accomplish. Unlike a vision statement that will need to be refreshed and modified periodically, a mission statement can exist forever.

Fire service leaders—lieutenants, captains, and chiefs—responding to an emergency create a vision based on the difference between the current situation encountered and the desired future situation, or conclusion of the emergency. The vision is the basis for the incident action plans that are developed to mitigate the emergency. It is through effective communication that the vision becomes a shared vision, providing a common destination that guides every firefighter striving to make order out of chaos at the emergency. The vision statement reflects desired future accomplishments and, as the vision becomes reality, the vision is refreshed with a new vision for future achievements. For firefighters, this represents the next alarm. What might a new vision represent in your world?

## People + Desire + Trusted Leadership = Teamwork

In the fire academy, the training captains would share their vision with the rookies every day. Each morning began with one of the captains addressing the training class. As the new firefighters stood at attention, the captain in question would recite his vision: "Each rookie graduates to firefighter status through the mastering of the skills and knowledge required!" This became the vision for the entire fire academy class. Every single rookie was striving to realize and to benefit from this shared vision.

There are many times in firefighter training, in business, and in life where events and situations become stressful and overwhelming. It is during these times that we must all remind ourselves of what we are trying to do and why we are trying to do it. The definition of success for the training process was part of the vision that had everyone united in what they needed to do and why.

Leaders are mentors, coaches, cheerleaders and, when necessary, disciplinarians. They provide the mission statement that will unite all involved. Leaders also provide the vision statement that will create the synergy to get the right things done by accomplishing the stated goals to realize future successes.

I can imagine that your business has an employee issue or two that are equivalent to a group of rookie firefighters going into a dark smoky basement or perhaps up and over some obstacle for the first time. When you need ordinary performance to rise to extraordinary performance, remember that desire is only the first step—albeit, a very important first step. Trusted leadership has the power to put people in positions to grow and develop by expanding comfort zones. Leaders will accomplish their performance goals for those who follow them when they provide vision and then mentor, coach, and cheer on these followers, when appropriate, by providing recognition for excellent performance.

Throughout the weeks of training, each rookie firefighter began to see himself as a member of the fire service family. We had learned a great deal about how firefighters do their work. We learned about the personal values that every firefighter is expected to possess. We also learned a lot about ourselves through the process that includes desire, conquering fear by getting outside of our comfort zones, building self-confidence, believing in a shared mission, understanding the vision, and gaining strength from group dynamics and teamwork.

Each rookie's own desire put that person at the crossroads of ordinary and extraordinary. The excellent trusted leadership that our training captains provided had inspired each of us to believe that we were firefighters who would soon be successfully responding, as part of a team, to extraordinary situations.

## What You Do Always Matters

One of the captains told us a story to illustrate something very important for every rookie to understand, regarding the responsibility that comes with a career as a firefighter. He pointed out that when someone has a leaky pipe, he or she may call two or three plumbers before deciding which one will do the necessary work. Usually, this is based upon who has the ability to get the job done, how much it will cost, and how soon the plumber can get to work on the problem. When that same someone needs help as they face potential disaster, a fire or life-threatening medical emergency, their call will be to 911. The caller will not have any say in who responds to the call for help. Sometimes, there isn't even time to think, just time to call 911!

The captain finished his story by saying, "As a firefighter responding to this call for help, each of us must be the best at what we do. How dare we be anything less?"

---

### 🔥 Hot Tip

Acknowledge the importance of what you do and how your daily efforts contribute to the overall success of the company or organization. Then think about why doing your job well always matters to someone.

Now ask yourself, *Who does it matter to?* Put a face on it. The answer will be different for everyone. Some may mention many people inside as well as outside of the organization, including themselves. Because families benefit when people are successfully employed, others might mention family members. Still others will say a coworker, client, society, or possibly their cat. It doesn't matter who they see as the beneficiary of their commitment to be the best. What does matter is that they make the commitment.

When you take personal ownership for doing your best, your best is what you will always try to do. If you're in a leadership position, take the time to have everyone on your team put a face on the person it matters to when that person does his or her job well.

---

This was a defining moment for every rookie who heard it. Isn't this the same motivation that would drive success in any business: the belief in a common purpose or mission? This is why firefighters spend a great deal of their time training and preparing for their next customer. Every firefighter knows what he or she does is important, and to do it well always matters to someone. Instinctively, firefighters put a face on who benefits when they succeed and who is hurt when they fail. This is an inspirational thought process that motivates each and every firefighter to want to be the best that he or she can be.

Anyone, in any line of work, will benefit from a culture that embraces such an attitude of engagement.

## Trust, Encouragement, and Opportunity

There was still one more major challenge every rookie had to accomplish prior to graduating from the fire academy. Once I saw it demonstrated, I realized that this would be a leap of faith, and there was a good reason that it was saved for last.

Every rookie must stand in an upper-floor window and step off with his or her feet and hands pointing to the heavens while falling, back first, into a rescue net (known as a life net) held by ten of their fellow rookies. It was a necessary task because, at that time, this was a rescue procedure that utilized a piece of equipment deployed by most metropolitan fire departments.

This was the ultimate game of trust. But this was no game! It was the culmination of everything we had accomplished. Intuitively, I was sure that it was so much more.

It was also the ultimate comfort-zone expander and thus a self-confidence builder. It would demonstrate my trust and respect for the abilities of those who would catch me and from those whom I would be part of a team to catch in return.

I remember feeling the fear as I stood on that ledge and looked out over the neighboring rooftops. I could even see the horizon off in the distance. Once again, we would have to deal with an unfamiliar situation, an activity that was located just outside of our comfort zone. I looked down, down, and farther down. I saw what appeared to be a very small round disc (actually about fourteen feet in diameter) being held by 10 people looking up at me, whom I recognized but couldn't remember their names, not to mention mine, at that moment.

But I knew if there were ever a situation where my choice was to jump into the life net or play the odds in an inferno, I would definitely take my chances with this leap of faith. I was thinking of the faith I had developed in those who had given me inner strength, encouragement to succeed, faith in our mission, and faith in the vision of becoming a Los Angeles firefighter. My thoughts were interrupted by the captain standing next to me, shouting, "Jump!" And that I did. My eyes fixed and looking up into the pale blue sky, it seemed like falling took forever. Then, just as planned, I landed on my back in the center of the net. After I landed safely, my fellow rookies dropped one side of the round net and rolled me off on to the ground. I jumped up and, still on an incredible adrenaline high, asked the captain if I could go again. He replied, "Sure, if anyone wants to jump again, go for it!"

Up the stairs I ran, along with other rookies. This time, standing on the ledge, I felt no fear, only desire and confidence. It is amazing to me how quickly fear melts away, only to be replaced by confidence with just a little trust, encouragement, and opportunity. I trusted in my leaders, they gave me encouragement, and the culture allowed me the opportunity to overcome my shortcomings to ultimately succeed.

I had achieved my dream. I couldn't wait for graduation day and to arrive at my first fire station assignment. I knew I still had a lot to learn, but there was nothing I wasn't prepared to try.

## To Be Successful at Anything, We Need Everything

One of the first things I noticed when I walked into my newly assigned fire station was the words emblazoned on the side of the fire engine and fire truck. Against the red paint, the words in white reflective letters stood out:

Class 1
Fire Department
City of Los Angeles

I asked my captain what "class 1" meant, and he pointed me to the fire station library to do some research to find the answer to my question (this was 1978, long before the Internet existed as we know it). I discovered that class 1 represented a very important and meaningful perspective of fire service culture. It is part of a rating system that is the responsibility of a nonprofit group known as the Insurance Services Office, commonly referred to as the ISO. This organization evaluates the effectiveness of the fire protection agencies throughout the United States for review by the insurance industry. The ISO uses a rating system that ranges from class 1 through class 10 (class 1 being the best, and class 10 being the worst, or nonexistent). The higher the rating a fire department receives, the lower the cost of fire insurance premiums for homes and businesses located within their response area.

For a firefighting organization to achieve a class-one rating is therefore an exceptional accomplishment and an acknowledgement that it is the best at what it does. This is a clear statement that officially defines a culture that is unique and represents a way of life. It reflects an organizational culture that is focused on success.

The Los Angeles City Fire Department was able to achieve and maintain the class-one rating. This was something to be very proud of. Our department received the authorization to display "Class 1" on every fire apparatus: trucks, engines, rescue ambulances, and so forth.

During a firefighter's career, receiving recognition for a task well done would sometimes elicit a compliment like, "Good job—that's class 1!" These types of references to a firefighter's performance by fire department leaders helps to infuse an attitude that embraces the value of continuous improvement, a feeling of accountability with empowerment to take appropriate actions, something that ultimately transforms the thinking of each new member of the organization.

We refer to this as the Class 1 Culture because it is an attitude that helps to create the individual's inspiration and motivation to be the best. These behaviors and recognitions definitely have a positive cultural impact, with elevated expectations on how people regard their work and themselves.

After many years of serving as a member of the fire service, having completed 16 years in the rank of captain, I had successfully responded to countless fires and other emergency situations—fires, floods, riots, and earthquakes. I experienced just about every type of emergency for which a firefighter is trained.

I was getting ready to head for home after a fairly quiet 24-hour shift. It was a beautiful and uneventful morning, when suddenly, as it always seems, the alarm sounded. The dispatcher's voice emitting from the station's speaker had an urgent tone as he said, "Structure fire." I heard the address and quickly placed the location in my head. It was a few blocks from the fire station.

The on-duty firefighters hurriedly responded. They were sliding down the firehouse poles from the second floor to the first floor, running toward the engine and the truck, and donning their heavy protective clothing: turnouts, gloves, and helmets.

I continued walking to the rear of the station. I looked out into the direction where the address was located to see whether there was any smoke showing. I heard the dispatcher say, "Woman reported trapped inside." I looked out and saw a column of black smoke rising into the sky. I hollered, "Loom up!" This is a firefighting term to describe smoke showing. Then I quickly got into my car and drove toward the scene of the fire, thinking, *at least I could watch the action.*

I was able to drive out of the parking lot at the rear of the station and then directly to the address. Because I didn't have to take time donning all of the protective equipment, and because the way the streets were configured, the fire apparatus had to go through a maze of residential streets to get there, I was able to arrive on scene first.

I ran to a small guesthouse behind the main house. I saw thick black swirling smoke coming from the front door. With the door already open, flames were lapping out from the top of the doorway. The smoke had banked down to the floor as it swirled angrily through the doorway like a black-and-gray tornado. As I approached, I saw a man kneeling in the doorway with a garden hose in one hand as he stared into the doorway. It was apparent that he was a neighbor who had responded to the fire wearing shorts, no shirt, and with shaving cream on his half-shaven face.

I ran up to the door, knelt to the man's left side, and asked, "Is there someone inside?"

He replied in a frustrated way, "Yes, but it's too hot to go in!"

While reaching for the garden hose grasped in his right hand, I said, "I'm a firefighter . . . give me the hose—I'm going in!"

"So am I! I'm telling you, it's too damn hot. I've already tried to go in!"

He was another off-duty firefighter with a mission to save lives. Our instincts told us to get low, below the heat and smoke, and follow the wall with one hand while searching with the other. I felt the extreme heat. The smoke was heavy, thick, and choking. I could only think, *Damn, it is too hot! If only I could see something or someone through the smoke!* This situation seemed so incongruous to me. I needed to get in there, and I couldn't. Deep inside of me was a class-one attitude to do my best, but it wasn't enough to overcome the challenge of the searing heat and suffocating smoke.

I could hear the sirens getting closer. Soon, the firefighters responding from my station arrived, quickly pulling a firefighting hoseline toward the doorway. As they momentarily stopped their forward progress to don their face masks and hook up to their SCBAs, I confirmed that there was reportedly someone still inside. They gave me an affirmative nod as they pulled up their protective hoods. And then, placing their helmets back on their heads, they secured them with a tug on their chin straps. Pulling the hoseline, they made their way into the smoke that seemed to swallow them whole. On hands and knees they crawled, following the wall with one hand while searching with the other.

Within a few minutes, they reappeared, dragging a woman out to the waiting paramedics. The woman was unconscious and severely burned from head to toe, her skin hanging from her naked body; her clothes had been consumed by the fire. I thought of the extreme pain she would endure if she survived—death might be a blessing. I could only imagine that if I had gone inside the way that I was dressed, I would have surely succumbed to the same fate.

For the first time since becoming a firefighter, I felt helpless. I stood back and watched as additional firefighters arrived to extinguish the fire. I looked at all the bystanders watching the action and, just like me, looking on helplessly. I had experienced the desire to go in and try to rescue the woman. I thought of the mission of the fire service: to save lives and protect property. I had the desire to do just that, but I couldn't.

As a firefighter, I am an ordinary person with special training, protective clothing, and equipment that allows me to work as part of a team to respond to extraordinary situations. I witnessed the on-duty firefighters quickly and courageously do exactly that.

Even though I had been responsible for training firefighters for many years, that day, I had been reminded of what my fire academy leaders had known as they set out to create a new group of firefighters: To be successful at anything, we need everything. It is impossible to rise from ordinary when the extraordinary situation presents itself, if all we have is desire. Desire alone is not enough. It is only the first step in a process that successfully shapes ordinary people like you and me.

It is not the ordinary person who becomes extraordinary. Rather, it is the right leadership creating the right culture that allows ordinary people to be capable of extraordinary outcomes, thereby providing all that is necessary to succeed. We do believe that there are exceptional individuals in every profession. But exceptional people will do extraordinary things regardless of the type of culture or leadership that exists. It should be the leadership's vision in every organization to improve the performance of every member—to provide what it takes to be the best that they can be.

A Class 1 Culture cannot exist without inspirational leaders, and together, they serve to empower ordinary people to become capable of extraordinary outcomes. This happens when everyone has everything he or she needs to meet the unique challenges that must be met in every type of profession and organization. Much like the fire service principles we have highlighted in this chapter, every organization needs leaders with vision, a mission to believe in that guides thinking and actions, learned skills, and tools of the trade. We all need the support and synergy that comes from teamwork. We need and appreciate a culture of trust, encouragement, and the opportunities to develop self-confidence and courage. With these critical principles in place, every business, organization, or occupation will have the ingredients for continuous improvement to achieve extraordinary results.

With inspirational leadership, you will be able to enjoy the benefits of a Class 1 Culture. Profit from it as you inspire others to successfully respond when the extraordinary situations happen. And they happen in all of our lives, every day.

## Chapter Review: Improve Your Process

The business relevance for this chapter is that every business task, profession or position requires the same evolution of human development that is necessary for the making of firefighters. Not the actual experiences that firefighter rookies must endure, but the cultural process from the fire service coupled with the experiences that someone in your company, organization, or vocation must have to possess the psychological and physical tools required to succeed.

When any workforce believes what they do is important and that doing it well always matters to someone, they will have the best opportunity to go from ordinary performance to extraordinary performance. This defines the Class 1 Culture.

Ensure that the following cultural principles are alive and well throughout your sphere of influence:

- Expand Comfort Zones: With the appropriate guidance and safeguards, people can reach new levels of performance, professional growth, and trust in leadership.
- Ordinary to Extraordinary: Create the expectation that everyone is continuously improving, incrementally, every day.
- Inspirational Leadership: Leaders must earn trust to become influential. This influence will serve to convince and inspire others to believe that achieving difficult goals is possible.
- Up and Over: Realistic training is important for people in all occupations and professions as they strive to be the best that they can be. People naturally fear the unknown but will look to trusted leaders for competence and trusted guidance to overcome any obstacle.
- Teamwork: The group or team dynamic provides each individual an inner strength. This is teamwork that comes from trust and mutual respect. Remember, no one wants to fail those whom he or she trusts and respects.
- Mission to Motivation: Every organization needs a common mission statement that provides all involved with a foundation for thought and guidance for action. It must speak to your organization's core reason for being. It must

be meaningful and memorable so that your people actually use it to motivate their thinking and their actions.

- Share the Vision: The vision that shows the way to future accomplishments sees the future. This allows leaders to create a culture that is working on the right things. They must provide a vision that illustrates, to every individual in the organization, how each one can contribute to making the organizational vision a reality.
- What You Do Always Matters: Tell the stories of what your business does for your customers, your clients, and your employees. Be certain that your people hear and understand that what they do and how they do it has an impact on others, on success, and on the future. Everyone should realize that doing his or her best always matters to someone.
- Trust, Encouragement, and Opportunity: Leaders must create an environment of trust, encouragement, and opportunity. These three ingredients will allow fear to melt away, only to be replaced by confidence, and confident people are successful people.
- To Be Successful at Anything, We Need Everything: Success requires leaders with vision, a mission to believe in and to guide our thinking and actions, tools of the trade, teamwork, and opportunities to grow.

## Revise: This Is Your Call to Action

1. What will you do differently in your work and in your life?
2. What is the size and scope of how you propose to improve?

## Notes

1. Firefighters' personal protective equipment includes boots, a heavy fire- and heat-resistant coat, pants, and hood (most commonly called "turnouts"), a helmet, gloves, and the SCBA that delivers life-sustaining air.
2. Rosalynn Carter, first lady of the United States, 1977–1981, date of quote unknown. BrainyQuote.com, http://www.brainyquote.com/quotes/quotes/r/rosalynnca126340.html, accessed July 30, 2014.
3. Jim Rohn, *The Treasury of Quotes* (Deerfield, FL: Health Communications, Inc., 1996), 72.
4. "Firefighting company" refers to a firefighting team, as in an engine company, truck company, and so on.
5. This was the LAFD mission statement until 2002, at which time it was changed by the governing administration of the City of Los Angeles. Many fire departments have followed a practice of expanding their mission statements, which arguably has rendered them less effective as a motivator for thought and action by their members.

# 2

# CPR for Business Success

*Let our advance worrying become advance thinking and planning.*

—Winston Churchill

With red lights flashing and siren wailing, the urgency was obvious as our fire truck raced through the streets of downtown Los Angeles. With a tremendous surge of adrenaline that started the moment the alarm sounded in the station, I thought about how far I had come in my training and personal development since my first days in the fire academy. Even though I was still considered a rookie firefighter with less than one year on the job and had so much more to learn, I was feeling fairly confident about being prepared for any task that might come my way.

I had this sense of confidence because of the organizational culture that put a huge emphasis on training the next generation of firefighters and future leaders. Training and development were a daily routine for every member of the fire department, not just for the rookies. Our mission as an organization was just too important to leave anything to chance. My thoughts were interrupted by the captain making a radio call to the emergency dispatch center.

The captain's voice was firm, yet calm, as he radioed, "Dispatch from truck nine: We have a loom-up." This meant that we could see smoke spiraling upward from afar, and our response was now to a working fire! The term "working fire," or "worker," was firefighter slang for a major emergency structure fire that would have everyone working hard to put it out. Since I was riding in a jump seat that faced the rear of the truck, allowing me to see only where we had been, I turned to get a look at what the captain was seeing. As I focused on the chaotic scene that we were rapidly closing in on, the dispatch radio crackled with the incident commander's (IC) voice.

It said, "Dispatch from battalion one. I am on scene and in command of a four-story center-hall apartment building with heavy smoke showing from the third and fourth floors. Give me a second and a third alarm."

As I was going through my mental checklist of all the things with which we might be tasked, I heard the IC give my company an assignment.

"Truck nine from IC, you have search and rescue on the third floor."

This was just one of the many tasks the IC was assigning to the arriving fire companies. Each assignment was part of his plan to achieve his vision for how these firefighting teams would work together to fulfill their common mission and to bring chaos to control.

Developing an incident action plan was the result of the IC sizing up the situation, which allowed him to identify all of the challenges this situation presented. It was now his duty to take command of this emergency and to be accountable for the mission of the fire service—to save lives and protect property.

My captain replied, "Roger, truck nine taking search and rescue on the third floor."

As the fire truck came to a stop, Mike (the firefighter sitting in the jump seat next to me) and I both stood up to strap on our axe scabbards. As we climbed off of the truck, I saw the captain talking into his radio microphone while motioning with his hand for Mike and me to come to him. Running toward our captain, we saw the scene becoming more chaotic as the apparatus operator and the tiller positioned the apparatus to put the aerial ladder up to the third-floor fire escape balcony (respectively, the driver of the ladder truck and the firefighter who steers the rear of the ladder truck's trailer).

In the midst of the multitude of firefighters arriving on scene, preparing for firefighting operations, some of the occupants were running out of the four-story apartment house, yelling to my captain.

"There's people still inside!" one woman screamed.

I looked up to see the cloud of thick black smoke continue to grow, billowing skyward from the upper-floor windows. I knew that if someone were still inside on the upper floors that he or she would not be able to survive for long. My captain had completed his own size-up to create a plan for our truck company to accomplish the assignments we were given by the IC. Concerned that any delay in beginning our search of the third floor could cost someone's life, the captain decided to send Mike and me as a team to start the search. The other members of our company were positioning the truck so they could utilize the aerial ladder (a hydraulically operated, 100-foot-long steel ladder connected to the fire truck). They would place the upper end of the ladder onto a fire escape balcony in case firefighters, or occupants, would need to rapidly exit the building. This was a standard operating procedure (SOP) for ladder trucks at working fires.

Armed with our assignment, Mike and I quickly made our way up the stairs to the third floor. We opened the door from the stairwell and were immediately hit by extreme heat and smoke. As we quickly donned our SCBA facemasks, standing an arm's length apart, we realized that the smoke was so thick that it prevented us from seeing each other. The conditions inside the apartment building were evident as we quickly worked together to develop a plan to search all of the apartments on one side of the hallway first, and then we would come back, searching the apartments on the opposite side. This would allow us to exit the building the same way we entered it—another best practice that encourages firefighters to always know their way out of a situation.

We would alternate, with one of us searching the small apartment unit, while the other stayed in the doorway with a flashlight. The flashlight simply looked like a faint glow through the dark and dense smoke. However, critically, it serves as a beacon to show the searcher the way out.

Each of us tried to catch our breath as we rested in the doorway of every other unit, while the other searched, making the operation go as quickly as possible. This procedure also assured that we could conserve our air supply to make it last as long as possible. Our goal was to complete the entire search area that we had been assigned before running out of air.

Entering the apartment, I utilized the same search method that I learned in the drill tower and on which even seasoned firefighting veterans would routinely train. The procedure requires that the searcher crawls on hands and knees, staying as low as possible. This is because the floor is where the air is cooler, and any possible visibility is closest to the floor as well. It is also where most fire or smoke victims will be found. As I searched the apartment, I followed the wall with one hand while simultaneously searching the ground for victims with my other hand. It was so dark that I couldn't see much, and what I could see, I couldn't really tell what I was looking at. I was reminded of my fire academy captain's warning and directive when he said, "When you're inside a burning building, the smoke can be so thick. It is pitch black, and you can't see your hand in front of your face. You have to learn to see with your hands."

I was amazed at how thick smoke can be, making it seem like the darkest night when actually, outside of the building, it was the middle of a bright and sunny afternoon. This was followed by my thoughts focusing on how deadly smoke is. I took a quick look back toward the doorway, and seeing the faint glow of Mike's flashlight gave me confidence that my escape route was still there. Fresh air, and help, wasn't that far behind me. I could continue to move rapidly, searching the apartment while expanding my comfort zone a little further.

I bumped up against something; it was a bed. Looking at the top of the bed, I could faintly see a pile of laundry. I pulled my axe out of its scabbard and held the axe head in my right hand and then quickly probed under the bed with the axe handle. Because children have been known to hide under beds and in closets when they are lost and frightened, this maneuver allowed me to quickly reach all the way to the far side of the bed. It was all clear, and I again found myself looking at the pile of laundry. I heard that voice in my head say, *See with your hands.*

Before moving on, I reactively placed both hands on the laundry. I was startled! I found someone—a motionless body.

I hollered to Mike, who was still in the doorway. "I found someone! I've got a victim!"

Leaving the flashlight lying on the floor at the doorway, Mike ran to my voice. I had already picked up the victim, and Mike grabbed the lower torso and legs. Together, we made our way back to the beacon and then down the smoke-filled hallway, down the stairs, and finally to the sidewalk outside.

Once safely away from all of the firefighting activities, we gently placed onto the sidewalk what we could now see was a young lady about 14 or 15 years old. As I checked for a clear airway and a pulse, Mike ran to get the oxygen bottle.

The command post was within 50 feet of our location, so I yelled to the IC that we needed a rescue ambulance, and the chief replied with a thumbs-up. Mike and I began working together to resuscitate our young female patient. We acted quickly to provide the pressurized oxygen that she would need to survive, delivering it through a mask that covered her nose and mouth.

Within a few minutes, the paramedics arrived to assist. The young woman began to move and regain consciousness. She slowly opened her eyes, looked up, and appeared to be focusing on us. Without warning, she jumped to her feet and began cursing at us while making derogatory hand gestures as she stumbled away. We all looked at each other with an expression of "What the —! What just happened here?" The paramedics ran after her and talked her into allowing them to take care of her. They gently placed her on their gurney and continued with appropriate emergency medical treatment with a quick ride to the trauma center.

We later discovered that this young woman had suffered a brain injury as a result of inhaling an excessive amount of toxic smoke. When she regained consciousness, the first thing she felt was a terrible headache. She was confused, disoriented, and incoherent, undoubtedly wondering who we were and why we had her on the ground in the first place. At that time, she had no knowledge of what had happened to her or how she had come so close to death. Certainly she wasn't aware of the fact that she was the main focus of so many decisions and actions by so many firefighters of all ranks who had responded to this fire emergency.

Even though none of the firefighters working on scene knew that this young woman existed, she was one of the reasons why the IC made his decisions, why my captain made his decisions, and why Mike and I made our decisions. We were all fulfilling our common purpose, our mission as firefighters.

While the occupants were fleeing in panic from the fire and smoke, Mike and I were inspired to run into the burning building. Aside from following orders, what inspired us to do such a thing? It was the belief that each of us had in the mission. We were inspired by cultural expectations for each of us to contribute to the IC's vision for the abatement of this emergency. Our shared values also provided us with complete confidence in our training and experience, which taught us that someone whom we had never met or even knew existed might need our help—someone like this young woman. Once we received our assigned task from our captain, we knew that what we were about to do was important. We needed to move quickly because, as always, doing our best just might matter to someone. In this situation, doing it well mattered immensely.

Firefighting is hot, dirty, and dangerous work. Because firefighters are ordinary people, they need to have distinctive processes to successfully respond to extraordinary situations. These processes have been developed to keep them from falling prey to noise, distractions, and competing priorities—all of which are present in various forms and degrees at emergencies. There is a simple set of principles that allows them to improve their process to be accountable, empowered problem solvers and to stay focused on the task at hand.

These principles come from our many years of firefighting and leadership experience. We have adapted them to provide your business with a strategic thought process that enables conceptual thinking and informed decision making. They are management, leadership, and success principles we call CPR for Business Success, as this chapter is titled.

What do you think of when you hear the abbreviation "CPR"? Right now, you are most likely thinking about cardiopulmonary resuscitation. That kind of CPR is important, and everyone should know how to perform it when necessary. But we need you to start thinking differently when you hear those three letters. This is because CPR for business represents three steps to success in whatever you are doing.

If the purpose of that other kind of CPR is to create a pulse by maintaining the flow of blood to sustain life, then the purpose of CPR for business is to always have your finger on the pulse, possibly to sustain the life of your business, to maintain the flow of success. CPR for business is a strategic thought process, represented by three steps as simple as: command, plan, and respond.

## 🔥 Hot Tip

CPR requires leaders at every level to take command of their situation. It empowers individuals and teams to deliver high-performance results by making good decisions to get the right things done for the right reasons and at the right time.

Facing tough situations is what firefighting is all about. Building your confidence in making the difficult decisions in your everyday, rapidly changing work environments is why CPR for business has been forged from the unforgiving world of firefighting. Having been fire tested, this powerful principle of firefighting management, leadership, and success has already proven to be a secret to success for personal and business accomplishments.

With CPR for business, you will confidently take *command* of every challenge that comes your way. You will always have a *plan* that includes the what-ifs to ensure that your vision of success becomes a reality. And finally, *respond* to your plan with what we refer to as a "Will-do!" attitude, or style, to signify that success is your focus. This is because in firefighting, lives are hanging in the balance, and properties are in danger of being destroyed. With such serious business in the works, firefighters can't just believe in can-do, they must believe in will-do. This is because everything they do is important.

Everything you do is also important, and whether you are launching a career, planning a business venture, or building a team, success should always be your focus. The following definitions for the three success steps of command, plan, and respond are now your focus. Improving your processes throughout your organization will become easier by thinking differently, with CPR for Business Success.

Let's take a look at what it means to live by the management, leadership, and success principles command, plan, and respond.

## Are You on Scene and in Command?

What would it take to inspire you to run into a burning apartment building when everyone else is fleeing in panic from the fire and smoke? There is definitely something exhilarating about hearing the alarm, sliding down the fire pole, dressing for success by getting into turnout gear, and riding on a powerful fire truck as it weaves through traffic. Your adrenaline flows with a sense of urgency as you realize that your purpose is to save people from violent harm or even death.

As entertaining as that may sound to some, we wouldn't really want to have you or anyone else actually run into a burning building unless you were trained and equipped for what you were about to experience. Similar to the fire service, success in your business is no accident, and what you must do to meet performance expectations always matters.

The following is the first of three steps that each of us must take to be successful at whatever we are doing: command. In business, the term "command" is rarely used. However, the need for guidance, direction, and clear communication is just as important to achieving business success as it is for firefighters working to extinguish a major fire. This initial step gives meaning to the phrase "taking command."

When the battalion chief had arrived on scene at the apartment fire, he announced over the radio, "On scene and in command." This message accomplished an important first step to pull together all resources involved into an organized and coordinated team effort. This simple statement by the incident commander defines the chain of command; identifies the management and leadership for deciding operational priorities; and establishes channels of communications, the methodology to acquire necessary resources, and the authority for all future directives. Those five simple words serve to inspire the behaviors necessary to get the process started off the right way.

However, no one would expect his or her CEO or team leader to walk into the office on Monday morning and proclaim in a thunderous voice, "[insert immediate supervisor's name here] on scene and in command!" If this were to happen, you might begin to believe that the stress of the job had pushed him or her over the edge. However, as firefighters, we wouldn't think that. Where we come from, this statement would seem very natural. That being said, it is important for everyone at every level of the organization to think and to act as though he or she is on scene and in command. We all need to take command of everything we do, from the small and routine tasks to the complex and critically important aspects of our professions and positions.

The following defines the five critical actions necessary for thinking and acting as though you are on scene and in command.

## Critical Action One: Situational Awareness

Have you ever been in a situation where you wanted to make a decision, but it didn't feel comfortable and you weren't absolutely certain? Therefore, you struggled along without making a decision. Or maybe you weren't sure what to do, but you made a decision based on assumptions, and it turned out to be a poor decision. This would be bad enough if you were going solo, but what if you were the leader of a team? If you had been trying to decide the appropriate actions for your team to take, this indecisiveness could have caused a great deal of uncertainty and possibly ultimate failure.

The obvious and distinct difference between firefighting and business is the actual work environment. The manner in which CPR for Business Success applies to your work is purely a matter of perspective. Think of the fire situation at the beginning of this chapter. Every firefighter at every level needed to have situational awareness for the assigned tasks. By feeling accountable for taking appropriate actions, each individual was focused on getting the right things done.

Consider the situations that you routinely encounter. Isn't situational awareness the first step in decision making? It also happens to be the first step in taking command of the situation. It necessitates knowing as much information as possible about the type of situation you are dealing with and whatever resources (people, things, money, and time) you will need and are available to deal with and improve that situation.

To demonstrate the business capacity of this process, let's look at customer service, for example. When taking command of a customer-related situation—internal or external—remember that customers want their problems solved. Always ask questions to understand the situation that has caused the customer's problem and to find out what resources the customer is willing to commit to the solution. Answering these two questions will put you on the right path to provide Class 1 Customer Service.

Having situational awareness also means to be present. Not necessarily physically present, but present in knowing and understanding the problems, obstacles, and challenges (POC) that you and your team currently has or will encounter.

Much like the decisions that were made at the apartment fire, making good informed decisions requires that you first become aware of the situation. In the same way, to take command of a task, occupation, or position, you must always understand the situation and know what resources are available for you to apply for the improvement of the situation.

## Critical Action Two: Two-Way Communication

When the fire chief announces that he or she is on scene and in command, the action of taking command starts the communication process. Two-way communication begins with this announcement, which requires that all leaders under the chief's command begin to listen carefully to what is being said.

The same is true for business leaders. Because poor communication and misunderstandings are the cause of so many organizational problems, these principles of improved communications are necessary in every type and instance of communications. This includes face-to-face verbal communications, any type of written communications (e-mails, letters, business proposals, etc.), phone calls, announcements on a public address system, voice mails, and so on.

Two-way communication requires that we speak and then listen, and listen and then speak. It is impossible for anyone to successfully speak and listen at the same time. Inadequate communications happen all the time, especially in stressful or unfamiliar situations, and they should not be tolerated.

It is always important that communications are accurate, succinct, and disciplined—to the point. Accuracy is most important; concise statements are beneficial; and clarity of the source of information is imperative. To encourage accurate two-way communications during stressful firefighting situations, the acronym PPN is employed. Translated, it means to state your current *position*, your current *progress*, and your current *needs*.

Leaders who have delegated numerous tasks at an operating emergency incident—or during an extensive business initiative—need assistance from team members for accurately consolidating messages and information. PPN provides a structured method, especially during rapidly changing situations, to do just that. It is everyone's responsibility to continuously practice improved communications. Utilizing the principles of two-way communication with PPN is a great way to start.

Another important cultural significance to two-way communication is that there is an exchange of ideas and information. Innovative ideas, opinions, or thoughts do not only flow one way. Successful two-way communication always flows in both directions.

It is a common situation for an incident commander to assign firefighting teams to a task in a location that is beyond their view. Once the firefighting team leader is physically in the necessary location to accomplish the assigned task, he or she will communicate to the commander a description of the situation at the assigned location. This exchange of information along with possible suggestions may ultimately change the strategy and tactics being employed by the IC.

The principal reason for the two-way exchange is to ensure that team leaders do not become blindly obedient to the radio commands of their sector or incident commanders. To properly monitor the actual conditions at every level of the operation with the greatest probability of success, there needs to be a constant exchange of clear and concise communications. If this is beginning to sound like the communication challenges in your organization, have no fear; it should. Communication problems are found wherever two or more people come together; all the more reason to take command of the communications within your environment.

The fire service relies on two-way communications for efficient and successful firefighting and rescue operations as well as for firefighter survival. If firefighters become imperiled and become part of the problem, how then would it be possible to be effective in fulfilling the mission? When you think about it, two-way communication actually improves everything with which any organization is involved.

There is one last principle to consider regarding communications: We must always ensure that our message has been heard and understood and that we understand messages from others. Anyone sending messages should receive from the intended receiver an acknowledgment of his or her understanding of that message. If the sender does not receive this acknowledgment, then clarifying questions should be asked and repeated until it is assured that the message was received and truly understood. If you don't ask for feedback, you can't be sure that your message was received and understood. This acknowledgment pertains to all types of communications previously listed.

### Critical Action Three: Define Success

Firefighters understand that when they are fighting a fire, success is defined as achieving a knockdown. This is a term used to describe the initial extinguishment of the advancing flames. As previously stated, for firefighters working inside a burning building, tasked with fire attack or search and rescue, seeing anything is very difficult. Understanding the definition of success prior to entering a burning building allows firefighters to engage whatever problems, obstacles, or challenges (POC) the situation presents to achieve success. Defining success for their team is a critically important step for team leaders.

When Mike and I received our assignment to perform search and rescue on the third floor, we knew that the definition of success was to complete that task as quickly as possible. Even if there were no occupants needing to be rescued, our quick completion of the search was our focus. This is because our leaders had shared the definition of success for a search-and-rescue operation during training as: speed, effectiveness, and response with a sense of urgency to complete the task. This was also a cultural norm throughout the organization.

In business, people need the same sort of definition of what success looks like. This is because things can get just as difficult to see when what we are trying to accomplish is not clear. Without the leader's input, most people will define success according to their personal opinion. When this occurs, the result is many individuals working towards very different and unrelated outcomes. Clearly, this is not the manner by which the team concept is intended to operate. Furthermore, when clarity is lacking, leadership is lacking.

Leaders must always define success before engaging any opportunity. This is because success is very hard to find if you don't, first, know what it looks like.

### Critical Action Four: Set and Prioritize Goals

Think back to the chaos of this chapter's opening scenario. Can you image what it must be like trying to function in that type of situation? Too often, competing priorities, noise, and distractions will cause people to lose focus on the intended goals. In business, losing focus can result in lost opportunities. Knowing the goals in priority order reinforces what needs to be accomplished to find success. For your people who are facing difficult and stressful situations, this information provides them with the confidence to make informed decisions to get the right things done for the right reasons and at the right time.

Always remember, for the best chance of achieving goals, they must be specific, measurable, achievable, realistic (or as firefighters might say, survivable), and timely.

## Critical Action Five: Be Accountable

Get things done and take ownership for the results, good or bad. Feeling that you are accountable means you are accepting your duty to serve. The fire service could not function successfully without a high degree of accountability. Firefighters have a culture that relies on accountability for all involved in order for principles like mission, vision, and values to actually have meaning and significance. This understanding is embedded in the fire service culture through an ongoing expectation from leaders regarding the importance of accountability. During the apartment fire, the IC was accountable for all of his decisions, my captain was accountable for all of his decisions, and Mike and I were accountable for our decisions. At very different levels of the organization, we all went to work and did the best we could because we took ownership for everything we did.

To improve accountability in your company or organization, there must be a cultural acceptance and the expectation that everyone takes ownership for what he or she does. How your leadership can make this happen is written throughout this book, as all of these fire-tested and business-proven principles are coupled together to form a Class 1 Culture. A great place to start to improve accountability is to provide the right mission, vision, and values so that your people know what they are accountable for.

### 🔥 Hot Tip

CPR for business offers management, leadership, and success principles that provide people with a strategic thought process to be accountable and empowered problem solvers.

## Taking Command of Your Business

When you think about it, the command step allows you to encounter the current situation, including resources that are available, and then visualize what must be accomplished to improve that situation. The size or type of the situation doesn't matter, but by looking at the things that you want to improve and then defining success and setting and prioritizing goals, you can deliver future improvements. What you have done is to create a vision for an improved future situation. Taking Command of a situation is having the vision to solve problems. Command is vision.

Remember, every situation encountered must include the resources to be considered. The person running the numbers, the chief financial officer or accountant, provides a dose of reality to your vision. This is where resource availability is introduced into your desired future situation.

What might happen if someone did not utilize a strategic step like command? I heard about a business leader who took over the top spot of a mid-size company. He was a very accomplished individual—well-educated, with a great deal of experience in business—who was friendly and personable; he seemed to have it all.

He quickly took control of the financials and developed a plan to correct the budget problems that he had inherited. His plan didn't get very far before he was met with fierce resistance every step of the way and from every level of the organization. The problem was that he had not considered what it would take to sell his ideas. More importantly, he had not taken the time to go out and get to know the people from whom he would rely on for ultimate success. He had failed to take command of his new position of being the CEO and company leader.

If he had known about CPR for Business Success, he would have taken the time to not only know the current financial situation but also know the current overall situation, to include all of the resources (people, things, money, and time) that were dedicated every day to the success of the company. Because this leader failed to know and to fully understand the POCs that he and his entire team faced, most members felt unappreciated and did not trust him. This is because at that point in his tenure, they did not know him. They were not willing to accept his cost-cutting measures because they felt that he did not have their best interests in mind.

His approach was to incorporate profound change without providing a clear understanding of where he wanted to take the organization. Uncertainty was on everyone's mind, as they felt a sense of betrayal. This was because he had not practiced two-way communications. It was only his ideas and information that flowed one way—top down—with no display of appreciation for anyone else's input. It is very important to take some time to actually get to know your human resources, to fully understand what they do, to let them know more about how you think, and to share your vision.

By not utilizing a process like CPR for business and, specifically, the command step, even accomplished leaders can fail at being accepted as a trusted inspirational leader. What troubles can be prevented in your organization with this strategic thought process that has been fire-tested and business proven? Both firefighting and business organizations require leaders who know how to take command and to lead with vision.

My coauthor, Jim Bird, distinguished himself while working in the Fortune 500–sector by following the principles found in this book. Bird was known for taking command of business situations, much like he had done during his firefighting career. Mike Voaden, senior director of national accounts for Beiersdorf Inc., worked with Bird for many years. Here are Mr. Voaden's thoughts on how well these fire-tested principles worked for Bird:

> I considered Jim to be a foremost expert in his unique field of the CPG industry. His passion, perseverance and code of ethics make him an exceptional business professional. His body of work in the LA [City] Fire Department complimented the business skills over his career at Alberto Culver.

Now that you have mentally positioned yourself on scene and in command and in full view of your vision for a desired future situation, your next step is to develop a plan that will ensure your vision for success becomes a reality.

## SIZE-UP a Plan to Realize Your Vision

To the untrained eye, firefighting can sometimes seem like a free-for-all attempt that includes a series of disconnected and chaotic actions aimed at hopefully extinguishing the fire. In reality, there is always a plan, and it is being implemented in an organized and coordinated fashion.

To take command of a situation, a three-alarm fire, an organization, a division, a project, a sales team, a customer, or yourself, it is imperative to provide a vision for all involved. This is the only way to ensure that everyone will know how to contribute to making your vision a reality. Remember, when you take command, you are creating a vision for a desired future that can now be seen out in front of you. Metaphorically speaking, it is out on the horizon, just waiting to be realized. In the *plan* step of CPR for Business Success, your task is to create a plan to achieve your vision.

Think back to that question we asked about the burning building. What would it take to inspire you to run in while others are running out? If you were going to dash into the unknown, wouldn't you want to know what you were trying to accomplish? Wouldn't you want to know that there was a plan to follow?

When everyone involved understands what the definition of success looks like and understands the goals in priority order, it is easier for him or her to take action. This is especially true when that action is difficult and is accompanied by an element of risk. By taking command, you are establishing your vision. Similar to the process used by the fire chief, you now need to develop the plan to make it all happen.

You are standing in the current situation. Think of your vision for success. See it out on the horizon. With the planning process that we are sharing here, you will be able to identify what is standing in your way that must be solved, hurdled, or overcome to realize your future vision. The key to a successful plan: a planning process that focuses on identifying the actual issues that must be dealt with to succeed.

Firefighters use a planning process that is known as a "size-up." We refer to this as the SIZE-UP Planning Process. It is a targeted and systematic approach for developing the right strategy and tactics that will ensure the realization of your vision. Once you know what you want or need to accomplish, this process allows you to quickly identify the POCs that stand between the current situation and your desired future situation: your vision.

Every firefighter, from the newest rookie to the seasoned fire chief, will complete a size-up during emergency operations. Each uses the same process from their different individual perspectives, and so can you. The following defines the six ingredients that go into the SIZE-UP Planning Process. First we gather the facts, and then we create our plan. To help you remember these critical planning ingredients, we have made it into an acronym that spells SIZE UP.

## See, Situation, Size and Scope

As you gather information for your plan, you either see it with your own eyes or through the eyes of someone you trust, and you must continuously maintain situational awareness. This is because the current situation has the potential to change, possibly causing you to change your strategy or tactics and even your entire plan. You must also be aware of the size and scope of each POC that you discover.

The fire chief in command of the apartment fire was not physically located where he could see all of the actual problems that needed to be dealt with. He needed to rely on others to expeditiously gather information and report their findings to him. My captain would eventually report that the fire victim had been rescued but that another fire company would be needed to complete the search of the third floor, as Mike and I were not able to complete our assigned task due to our rescue efforts.

There were times when, as a battalion chief in command of a reported high-rise office-building fire, I would need to determine if the responding engine and truck companies will encounter an actual fire burning on the 20th floor or if we had responded to a false alarm. With no smoke or flames showing from my vantage point, I would need to verify what I was dealing with before I could develop my plan of attack. I could make some basic assumptions to get essential operations started, but I didn't want to base a plan exclusively on assumptions. Plans based on assumptions have a high failure rate.

A good example of this is the earlier story of the new CEO who ran into difficulties with his entire company. Even his leadership team pushed back on his plan because he based the cost-cutting phase on assumptions that were developed without the team's input. By coming into a new leadership position and not taking the time to complete the command step, he was forced to assume how the workforce would react to not only the plan but also—more predictable and preventable—to his lack of leadership. He did not know and understand the POCs that the operational level of the company was dealing with, thus resulting in much of the CEO's plan being based on assumptions. This individual was a very intelligent and accomplished executive, but his lack of situational awareness for the operational side of the organization made him seem out of touch.

Therefore, I would see the situation and know the extent of the POCs through the eyes of the fire attack team. As the team walked the stairs all the way to the 20th floor, and beyond if necessary, they would investigate throughout their ascent. They would make successive reports to my command location, keeping me apprised of what they discovered about the current situation.

My plan would be developed based upon the outcomes of this two-way communication, utilizing effective communication principles such as PPN. This same situation can occur in business, especially where team leaders—department directors, managers, and supervisors—aren't physically located with their team members. This is often the case for sales forces, buyers, and a multitude of other organizational workforce structures.

## Information

In addition to fire-related assistance, firefighters provide life-saving emergency medical services (EMS) for our communities. Firefighters are sometimes assigned to a rescue ambulance instead of an engine company or truck company. On one occasion, it was my turn to ride on the rescue ambulance for a 24-hour shift. We received an emergency call to an old but fairly upscale apartment building located on the west side of downtown Los Angeles. The dispatch information we received was to respond to a DB (dead body). We responded with red lights flashing and siren wailing. Upon our arrival, we immediately checked in with the desk clerk, who was standing at the check-in counter located in the first-floor lobby.

The clerk told my partner and me in a mournful voice, "Mr. Jones is upstairs in his bed . . . dead." He went on to explain, "Mr. Jones has come down to the lobby to read the paper every evening for the past eight years. Tonight he never showed up, so I went to check on him, and sure enough, he's dead."

We asked for his assistance, and the desk clerk obliged by leading us to Mr. Jones's apartment. We arrived, and the clerk hesitantly slid the key into the lock and slowly opened the door. Before walking through the doorway, my partner said, "Okay, don't touch anything, because this might be a crime scene!"

As we slowly entered the apartment, we didn't turn on the lights, and my partner fumbled for his flashlight. We walked down a small entry hallway, and the only light we could see came from an old black-and-white television set. It was glowing in the corner of the room with the sound turned down to where we couldn't hear it. We slowly walked to the bedside and, with my partner's flash light now illuminating Mr. Jones, we saw that he had a sheet wrapped tightly around his upper torso and head. Because we had been sent to assess the situation and, in this case, pronounce the man dead, my partner gently grabbed the sheet with one hand and slowly started to pull it from Mr. Jones's head. With only the faint glow from the TV and my partner's dull, yellow-tinted flashlight beam on Mr. Jones's sheet-covered head, the whole scene takes on an eerie feeling, as we were both curious what Mr. Jones's face looked like.

I was wondering, *Was this natural death . . . maybe a heart attack, or was there some sort of a struggle and we are now dealing with a homicide?*

The sheet softly slipped from the man's face. My partner and I moved in closer to get a better look when—the man's eyes popped open as he calmly asked, "Can I help you?"

With the exception of Mr. Jones, everyone in the room jumped in unison as if we had just seen a ghost. It turned out that Mr. Jones was just fine, but he had a touch of the flu and thought he'd skip his nightly routine.

If you only remember one thing from this entire book, please remember this: First we receive information, and then we receive accurate information. Never totally trust the first things you hear, and don't assume that you have all of the information available when developing your plan. The more information you can receive to identify your POCs, the better your plan will be.

## Zero In

Once firefighters have knocked down the flames, totally extinguishing the fire, and the smoke has cleared out, fire investigators will then dig through all of the charred remains to zero in on the exact location where the fire started. This spot is known as the "point of ignition" or "area of origin." This allows for the discovery of not only the cause of the fire but also what can be done to prevent this particular type of fire in the future.

As we gather information and specific knowledge for our plan, we all must try to zero in on the cause of the POCs that stand between our current situation and our future vision. We must prioritize the order in which each of the POCs will be encountered and mitigated. In firefighting, business, or our personal lives, understanding the cause of an issue is an important step to deciding how best to deal with it. This information allows us to develop the most effective strategies, solutions, and actions for a successful plan.

A very simple illustration of how zeroing in works would be a bucket that is being filled with water flowing from a kitchen faucet. If we don't want the bucket to overflow once the bucket is full, we can determine the best solution to solve our problem.

Because we know what is causing the water to fill the bucket, we have the right information to allow us to decide the best choice for preventing the bucket from overflowing. Do we: (a) Stand there all day and bail out the bucket? (b) Remove the bucket from the flow of water? or (c) Turn off the faucet?

As a coach and consultant for organizational culture and leadership, I utilize the SIZE-UP Planning Process to identify precisely what needs to be dealt with for my clients to realize their vision for improvement. One of my main areas of focus is to figure out what is causing the problems, obstacles, or challenges. Knowing the cause points us to the best solution every time.

## Environment and Exposures

This component is the practice of seeing the 360-degree view of everything that is affecting the situation. Firefighters consider every fire emergency to have six sides. Much like a box, there is a top, a bottom, and four sides. Everything inside the box is considered the environment. Firefighters must have a continuous and complete understanding of every possible effect that their actions, and the actions of the fire, will have on the environment in which they are working.

Knowing what to expect within our work environment ensures that we will always be dressed for success. For firefighters, this means to be prepared with protection from 1,500-degree heat and a poisonous atmosphere and to have techniques to deal with zero visibility. Your environment will hopefully be less dangerous, but it will most likely be just as important to know about for you to succeed.

In abating the emergency, firefighting teams must constantly consider who or what is being exposed. How are the firefighting operations, the fire, the smoke, and the hazardous products of combustion or water that is being applied inside the box affecting the exposures? People, their possessions, and all materials and properties outside of the box in all six directions are considered exposures. Firefighters protect these exposures through their coordinated efforts to confine the fire and its byproducts to the original environment inside the box. Even though a fire is confined to the original environment, who or what might be exposed is always being considered for protective actions.

We have found in business that functional silos can be compared to the fire environments. These silos can become very dysfunctional as the people involved begin to interact, or create exposures, with others outside of their own work silos. There are times when they don't speak the same business language, and this can cause communication problems to occur. This is an example of the environment being defined as a department or division that performs specific functions within a larger company. When those employees interact on shared projects with employees of other departments or divisions, an exposure of sorts has occurred, and mistakes can take place. This is usually due to communication failures and misunderstandings.

When being vigilant for potential POCs, either internally or externally, it may be very beneficial to think in the manner by which firefighters mentally approach every fire. Consider the six sides of your organization's environment and who or what is potentially being exposed to trouble. Much the same as out-of-the-box thinking, this is damage control at its core.

Firefighters are trained to be alert for the presence of POCs by physically looking up, down, and all around. You should get in this habit too, at least figuratively; look up, look down, and look all around your company or organization. As you gather information for your plan to achieve your vision, always be aware of the ongoing affects caused by your actions and inactions, the actions and inactions of your team, or the actions or inactions of your company. Put another way, how are your team's actions or level of performance affecting other associated business teams within your company? How is your organization's vision affecting your industry, your business environment, your competitors, your customers, or your employees?

## Uncover the Unknowns

For firefighters, surprises can be dangerous and sometimes deadly. In business, surprises can be dangerous, costly, or annoying and distracting at the least. When completing a size-up, we must try to uncover the things that we don't know. And guess what? We never know what we don't know.

Because of this, we must look deeper, uncovering the unknowns by asking questions of the appropriate people about what we do know. It's amazing what we can learn by asking the right people questions about things we think we know the answers to and then listening very carefully to their responses. When you do this, you will usually uncover things that you had not even considered.

A firefighting example of uncovering important unknowns using this process occurred at a seemingly innocuous garage fire behind a residential home. Firefighters approaching the garage initiated the size-up process for planning their fire attack. Heavy thick gray smoke was observed coming from around the large, locked, garage door and through the roof vents.

The firefighters asked questions of the residents regarding the presence of people that may be living in the garage and if a car were parked inside.

All of these questions were answered with a no. Without any such challenges to affect a routine firefighting operation, the firefighters went to work.

One of the firefighters with the task of forcible entry was searching the perimeter of the garage in an attempt to provide the most effective entry for the fire-attack team. In his search, he observed that outside and adjacent to the garage, there was piled an assortment of hunting gear, elk antlers, and empty ammunition boxes. The firefighter radioed the IC and reported this information.

The IC, now knowing this discovery, questioned the residents of the home. The IC's questions evoked answers that identified the residents' son as an avid hunter with a moonlighting business pertaining to custom ammunition loading and weapons sales. Additional questions revealed that the garage was overloaded with live cartridges, heavy-caliber ammunition, gunpowder, and other explosives.

The IC immediately halted the forcible-entry operation and the entry of the fire-attack team. An interior fire attack would be too dangerous, with the obvious potential of exploding ammunition. All personnel were directed to pull back to a safe distance, and a defensive fire attack ensued. Hoselines were coordinated by firefighters from outside of the garage to apply a large quantity of water into the garage.

The strategy and tactics were altered by the IC in time to prevent possible injury to the firefighters attempting entry for a direct interior attack on the fire. Hundreds of live cartridges could have been discharged, potentially causing a large explosion and possibly causing serious or fatal injuries to firefighters.

Uncovering the unknowns was accomplished at this emergency by just asking questions about known facts and then listening to the answers. In this incident, questions regarding information the firefighters already knew influenced additional questions, directed to the right people, regarding a situation that had not been previously considered.

In both business and firefighting, we have been in leadership positions that have a level of supervision and leadership between us and the workforce. Using such a technique helped us to stay connected to the technical side of the work performed and also served to uncover the unknowns that have little visibility to some leadership positions. Just by asking people questions about how their work is done and what their challenges are, thereby soliciting ideas for improvement, allowed us to learn about many issues that we had not even considered.

Try this technique in your business. You will become a better listener, and it really works.

## *Plan*

Having gathered and analyzed the available information, you must take the final step in developing an initial plan that will deliver success by achieving your vision. What gives this process the power to realize your vision? It is that you now know exactly who or what stands between your current situation and your desired future vision.

## Planning for Business Success

If you think of a plan as a road map, then you can have the confidence that this road map also shows where all of the road hazards (problems), detours (obstacles), and heavy traffic (challenges) are located.

Your plan will evolve depending on the situation, the available resources, and the known information. This process is not meant to stifle a quick response or action. To the contrary, it is designed to focus on discovering as much information as possible in a short period of time. The SIZE-UP Planning Process allows anyone to know enough to put a plan together, to take initial actions, and to begin to get things done.

Believe it or not, firefighters will utilize the SIZE-UP Planning Process in minutes, sometimes in seconds, to get ahead of a fast-moving emergency situation. Obviously, for firefighters, quick action can save the day. Also, there is rarely enough time to overly accumulate information and to experience what sometimes can occur in business: the dreaded information overload, better known as analysis paralysis. The key here is to know enough about your POCs to respond to the current situation based upon the information which is readily available. Even as you and your team put your plan into action, the information search should continue—the more information, the better—until your vision has become a reality.

What might be possible in your daily routine if you had hours, days, or even weeks to use this process and size up a plan for a business situation that needs to be improved? This process also works for planning a project, making a sales presentation, or facing other business development opportunities. In every case, we need to have a plan. But plans won't do anything until we put them into action and respond.

### Respond as Though It Matters—It's a Cultural Thing

Now that a plan is in place, it is time for all engaged participants to respond to that plan. The plan acts as a guide to bring the inspirational leader's vision to reality. This can only occur if the plan is well-communicated. Effective communication of the plan provides every person involved with necessary directives to respond correctly to the plan. Responding to the plan defines how each individual and each team will contribute to the realization of the shared vision.

> **🔥 Hot Tip**
>
> CPR for business creates a culture where people respond with a focused will-do attitude because they know that what they do is important, and doing their best always matters to someone.

When we talk about step three of CPR, we are really getting to the heart of a culture that is dedicated to strive for success and to be the best. We are talking about what motivates individuals and teams and why they respond the way that they do. This is where the Class 1 Culture is most evident in an organization and where inspirational leadership must be omnipresent. The following section defines the five cultural factors necessary for you to take the final step: respond.

### Cultural Factor One: Respond As Though It Matters

Firefighters have a culture that understands that everything they do matters. It may be a simple task, such as checking one's personal protective equipment daily to ensure everything works and is in its proper place. Or it might be responding as a member of a firefighting team with a sense of urgency to a 911 call for help. The small things and the big things all matter to someone.

The big things are usually obvious to spot, but the small things are much easier to overlook; to put it another way, they tend to fall through the cracks. If enough small things go unnoticed, big problems can be the result. For example, as a 16-year-old high school student, I worked at McDonald's. This was back when Ray Crock was the CEO, and he would occasionally be spotted driving through the parking lot of each restaurant. What was he doing? He was paying attention to the small things as he shared his vision for the success of the big things with the regional manager, who was usually at the wheel, driving him from restaurant to restaurant. Mr. Crock was personally demonstrating the importance of the small things as he looked at the way each restaurant was being maintained: litter-free parking lot, clean eating areas, neatly trimmed shrubs, sparkling windows, and so forth.

As a fire captain and fire station commander, I would similarly be constantly aware of the big things and the small things. The big things included preparedness and readiness for the next alarm. This was a daily routine that resulted in physical fitness, firefighting and rescue lectures, hands-on training, and of course the continuous oversight and guidance I provided during actual emergency situations.

The small things would include such duties as cleaning the station. Even though cleanliness might seem insignificant when compared to the big picture duties, it was no less important. After all, with so many people living within the fire station environment, maintaining cleanliness also provided the healthy environment necessary to ensure our organization would always be ready to respond with firefighters fit for duty.

On one occasion, the firefighting companies had just returned from an all-night fire. The apparatus and equipment were dirty, and so were the firefighters. Everything needed to be cleaned and readied for the next alarm. As luck would have it, on this particular morning, a group of dignitaries visiting Los Angeles City Hall was going to stop by to tour the fire station. This was a routine in Los Angeles because this particular fire station was located in Hollywood, and at that time it had the most resources on duty than any other fire station in the city. It was also a large, old, and historic building that today houses the LAFD museum.

As I was making my rounds to ensure that priority duties were being accomplished, I saw one of the senior engineers walking out of the first-floor restroom carrying a mop. The reason this looked odd to me is that this engineer had other things to do, and typically it was the rookie firefighters who would be performing such chores.

I stopped and asked, "Hey, Al, what are you up to?"

Al replied, "Well, Cap, I've got the kids changing hose on my engine, so I wanted to get this bathroom cleaned before the dignitaries arrived. If they saw this bathroom the way it looks after everyone had washed up, they might think we're a bunch of slobs!"

Wow, I was truly impressed. Not as much with the actual work performed, but with Al's reasoning that motivated him to respond the way that he did—with a mop.

In a similar situation, a company manager that I was consulting with told me about a business client that used the business's restroom and found that there were no paper towels. During their meeting, this gentleman took the time to point out that there were no paper towels in the restroom, and then he went on to speculate about what else the company didn't pay much attention to. Indeed, the small things really do make a difference. Based on the small things, how would your clients and customers rate your organization?

## Cultural Factor Two: Respond to the Plan

Inspirational leaders know the value of working as a team. They also know the importance of communicating with those who follow so they fully understand the plan. For any of us to respond effectively to the plan, we must also have knowledge of some other things. We must know the vision that we are contributing to. This includes understanding the definition of success and knowing the goals in priority order. If you are part of a Class 1 Culture, you need to get into the habit of asking yourself, "What are we trying to do, and why are we trying to do it?" If you don't know the answers, practice two-way communication and find out.

We have seen organizations or teams within organizations that are continuously in the planning phase. Unfortunately, they sometimes have a difficult time getting into the execution or responding phase. If your organization has this challenge, try this action step and respond to the plan, as it has been developed to focus on the success.

Whether leading an emergency response to fight for saving lives and protecting property or leading a business initiative to fight for market share—or any other organizational endeavor—the best prepared plan will not achieve the desired goals unless everyone involved responds to the same plan.

## Cultural Factor Three: Appreciate Everyone's Contribution

It is a human need to feel appreciated. I have never heard anyone say, "No one appreciates a thing that I do, and that's just the way I like it!" Future motivations can be inspired by demonstrating appreciation of someone's efforts and accomplishments. Teams must learn to show appreciation for the struggles, progress, and achievements of all involved by recognizing that everyone's efforts contribute to the team's success.

Even in firefighting, everyone doesn't get to "catch the baby" every time. Not all tasks are glamorous, but the glamorous ones aren't possible without the support of everyone doing his or her part and doing it well. Giving appreciation creates a positive workplace. Once appreciation is shared with others, it has a way of coming back to those giving it away. Our experience is that people who feel appreciated at work are motivated people, and motivated people are successful people.

## Cultural Factor Four: You Go . . . I Go Teamwork

In the movie *Backdraft*, there is a scene where one firefighter nearly falls into the fire, but to save the day, a team member grabs him by the hand. As the first firefighter dangles helplessly, the firefighter holding onto him says, "You go . . . we go." There are many things in that movie that are exaggerated, as Hollywood is known to do to make things seem bigger than life, but in this scene, we think they got it right.

We call it "you go . . . I go" teamwork: doing better by working together. High-performance teams never have the option of throwing up their hands and deciding that something is too difficult, that they're too tired, or that nothing can be done, so let's just go home and leave it for someone else to figure out. Firefighters and other high-performance teams go the distance because they go together.

Teamwork is one of the most important ingredients to developing the Class 1 Culture. It is also very dependent upon the impact of leadership to make teamwork happen. In my effort to develop a high-performance business team I was reminded that you go . . . I go teamwork can be a challenge if people don't trust, like, or respect each other.

During a meeting, I asked for opinions on a seemingly unprovocative topic and the conversation turned into a disruptive dispute between two peers. Because of some past misunderstandings and conflicts, these two associates were at odds about almost any issue that came up. Having CPR as a mental checklist, I could begin the process of becoming aware of whatever situation had caused this emotional explosion. In the moment, this took me directly to the respond step, to de-escalate the situation and redirect the group's focus by emphasizing teamwork. This included the need for us all to work as a team and to develop a plan to improve the issues we think are important. In other words, I was able to bring the focus back to success for the team.

You go . . . I go teamwork will be covered in much greater detail in chapter 4.

## Cultural Factor Five: Develop the Will-Do Attitude

A will-do culture exists when people want to make a positive difference. When people intrinsically believe in themselves and in what they do, they respond with a focused will-do attitude. They embody this culture by possessing a belief that what they do is important, and that doing it well matters. When an entire workforce believes this way, the members will actually hold each other accountable for this value system.

Think of it this way: When a firefighter is pushing up a heavy ladder to the side of a building, hand-over-hand, rung-by-rung, the closer the ladder gets to vertical, the harder the firefighter must push. This is the point that might cause some people to give up because it seems too difficult to continue. But there is a point where the weight of the ladder is suddenly repositioned, pushing down through the ground to provide a greater foundation. The situation now becomes more of a balancing act, requiring little further effort to safely lower the top of the ladder into place—success achieved. Instead of a ladder, think of any problem, obstacle, or challenge that you are struggling with. Usually, the most difficult point in completing any endeavor is just before the point when things become more balanced. This is one of the major benefits of the Class 1 Culture and the focused attitude that comes with it; will-do people don't give up.

It takes inspirational leaders actively showing their people what is necessary to make a difference in their work. Your people will be committed to the cause and will want to go the distance when they have learned to focus on success. For any organization wanting to thrive and to grow, developing the will-do attitude is an essential principle to infuse into the culture.

## What Will CPR for Business Do for You?

It all depends upon what type of organization you work in. What you do and why you do it will take on a different meaning in various industries. For example, let's say you work in health care within a hospital. The work is vitally important, yet many hospitals have a high rate of failure when it comes to patient-care issues. We have all heard the stories about the wrong leg being operated on, for instance. But even though most health care workers really do care about their patients and want to do their best work, sometimes the processes within a large medical facility can be the problem that takes away clarity to what is truly important. A strategic checklist for critical thinking could help improve a process that has become the problem.

Furthermore, because ordinary people can be adversely affected by a process that is unwieldy and confusing, leaders must work extra hard at developing situational awareness for such things. To improve your process, you must be constantly aware of where the failures are and assume that if one person has made the mistake, others will surely follow.

We all have those moments in life when things come at us so fast that we need to react, and we need react in the best way possible. In firefighting, the wrong reaction could be deadly; in business, it could be costly; and in life, it could be downright regretful. CPR for business will give you the ability to maintain composure and to take command of the situation, quickly size up a plan, and then respond to that plan with a focused will-do attitude. Utilizing principles as simple as command, plan, and respond provides us with a continuous thought process that acts like a mental checklist for critical thinking, especially during stressful situations.

I use the details in each of the three steps (refer to Figure 2.1) to map out a problem in my work on a whiteboard or with pen and paper. Going through this process helps me to see the situation as it truly is and then define what I want to do with the situation, develop a plan to get there, and decide who is going to respond to solve the problem or deal with the issue. I routinely do this with my leadership team. Together, we are able to find the best solutions by having everyone participate to have the same understanding of our challenge. Coupled with the knowledge and experience that my team members bring to the table, this process works wonders by focusing our attention on success.

What does it take to inspire anyone to run in while everyone else is running out? CPR for Business Success will provide the same inspiration and motivation for you and your business teams as it does for firefighting leaders

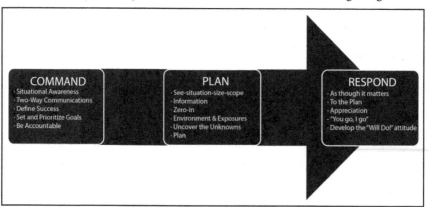

**FIGURE 2.1**

and their teams. These principles are simple enough for firefighters to use on the run, yet proven to be flexible enough, practical enough, and useful enough to be applied to most every business situation.

This is not theory. These are facts from real-life firefighting and business experiences and outcomes. These principles of management, leadership, and success can also apply to your business. Without these principles, firefighters wouldn't be consistently striving for success and, possibly, wouldn't survive in many situations. They have been adapted for your use and can provide your business teams with improved opportunities to succeed.

Make CPR for Business Success part of your process, and you will possess the power that comes from leaders, with an entire workforce that has the vision to solve problems and effective planning skills as well as an organizational culture dedicated to being the best.

## Chapter Review: Improve Your Process

How can CPR for Business Success serve to improve your process by providing every individual in your company or organization with a strategic success formula? Imagine that you, your peers, and your supervisors—everyone in your company or organization—had the power of critical thinking that CPR provides. How would CPR impact your business?

The main points: Everyone takes command of everything he or she does, ranging from the small and routine tasks to the complicated and critically important aspects of that person's occupation, profession, or position. There is always a plan to follow, and everyone responds to the plan with a focused will-do! attitude.

Adhere to the following guidelines to put CPR for Business Success to work for you and your organization.

1. Think and act as though you are on scene and in command with the vision to solve problems.
2. SIZE UP a plan for your success.
3. Respond to the plan with a focused will-do attitude.

## Revise: This Is Your Call to Action

1. What will you do differently in your work and in your life?
2. What is the size and scope of how you propose to improve?

# Creating Continuous Incremental Improvement

*Successful people form the habit of doing the things that failures don't like to do.*

—Albert E.N. Gray

Just before midnight, the alarm came in, and within 60 seconds, I was responding as part of a first-alarm assignment to a reported structure fire. As we approached the address, we could see some light smoke showing from the roof of a shopping mall. I announced this over the radio to the dispatch center and, simultaneously, to all of the fire companies arriving on scene and waiting anxiously for an assignment.

To my amazement, the fire began to grow, spreading rapidly into three retail stores. Within a few minutes, these three stores had become engulfed in flames. This fire had now become a major emergency. I promptly requested additional firefighting resources that equaled a third alarm. This situation had become serious business.

As the IC, I took command of the emergency with a heightened awareness of the current situation confronting all of the first responding firefighting resources. My primary actions were to open two-way communications with all levels of leadership now engaged in this firefighting operation. This allowed me to state my definition of success and to prioritize the goals necessary to achieve that success. It also allowed me to share my vision so that all involved could understand how this fire's destructive path would be stopped.

I then completed a size-up so that I could quickly develop a plan for attacking this fire. Following my plan, I directed the first responding fire companies to priority tasks. Each firefighting team and each firefighter within those teams would take a piece of the plan, responding with will-do style—a manner in which firefighters always respond when it comes to dealing with emergencies. These collective efforts would eventually contain the fire to the initially involved stores and then zero in on the seat of the fire to finally knock down the flames.

This fire was a difficult struggle for the 75 firefighters who responded as part of 18 different firefighting teams. Firefighters from truck companies provided vertical ventilation by cutting holes in the roof to let the smoke and heat escape the building. This is an important task that is carefully coordinated. It allows the engine company firefighters to work in safer conditions as they enter the building to advance hoselines and aggressively attack the growing flames. Simultaneously, other firefighting teams had forced entry by cutting metal doors open with power saws to provide access for the engine company firefighters, while still others were coordinating the breaking out of windows with axes to assist in ventilating the smoke and heat from the building. All of these actions by the various firefighting teams were in support of the overall plan that started with my vision for solving this problem.

There were some touch-and-go moments when I considered changing my initial strategy. This was due to the fire's stubborn nature and the subsequent difficulties that the firefighters had encountered during firefighting operations. Thankfully, the dynamics of the SIZE-UP Planning Process allowed me to maintain my overall vision with patience. I was able to recognize that prioritized tasks were being accomplished, and ultimately, the firefighters prevailed.

This was a valuable achievement. The majority of the shopping mall had been saved as well the many jobs that went along with each business that was in jeopardy. Other than the three affected stores, all other businesses went untouched by this fire. We had no injuries to occupants or firefighters, an outcome that is always great news.

Even though the majority of the shopping mall had been spared, the damage was significant—estimated to be $700,000. However, without vision to solve the problems encountered, two-way communications, a well-defined plan, and will-do attitudes to see it through, the loss could have been in the tens of millions.

Typically, once a fire is knocked down, the firefighters can take a much-deserved break before the cleanup starts, traditionally referred to as "overhaul." This period of time also gives the fire investigators an opportunity to carefully examine the charred debris to determine the cause of the fire.

While the fire investigators were busy doing what they do best, I would promptly develop a demobilization plan. The resources no longer needed for the overhaul were designated as available. This alerts the dispatch center as soon as possible when each fire company is ready for service and can be dispatched to the next alarm. But before I would release any fire companies from the scene, I needed to take one more, very important, step.

The fire service has a culture that reviews everything they do to maintain their commitment to continuous improvement. Therefore, I called all of the leaders to the command post for a postincident review. The captains from the engine and truck companies and the battalion chiefs who commanded divisions of the fire all came together as a group to briefly discuss this latest experience. Each individual leader had a turn to briefly discuss the actions of his or her team: what went right, what went wrong, and why.

This review process is one of the most important steps in further developing everyone involved within the organization. Because no one person has all of the answers, this review allows for a collective discovery of most of them. The fire service operates on the premise that as an organization, we are all in this together, and together we will ensure continuous improvement and personal development. This premise is foundational and is a cultural improvement that leads to continuous organizational success.

## How to Predict the Future You Want

Even with principles like command, plan, and respond, fires don't always cooperate, even with the best efforts by firefighters. The sheer destructive power of fire requires that the fire service have a process to continuously learn and improve from each experience. This is an important step for firefighters to become more effective at saving the lives and protecting the property of their customers while also surviving these trials by fire.

Subsequently, the fire service reviews everything they do, from a single-engine-company operation at a vehicle or small rubbish fire to all the companies working at a multiple-alarm fire or an entire department working at a major disaster. This process is conducted to ensure that continuous improvement is achieved when deficiencies are observed. It is also the way that the fire service develops best practices. Where improvement is possible for individual, team, and organizational performance, changes are formerly introduced into standard operating procedures (SOPs) and training practices.

We call this "$R^2$" to represent the review-and-revise process. In statistics, the coefficient of determination is $R^2$; it is used in statistical models whose main purpose is the prediction of future outcomes. What better way to accurately predict future business outcomes than to review everything you do to discover what went right, what went wrong, and why? When any organization adopts a process like $R^2$, it will experience immediate positive results.

## Review Is Where Your Profit Is

*Review* is the first step in the $R^2$ process and one of the most important steps in developing everyone within the organization. It represents a team effort for improvement, and it is a necessary step because experience alone doesn't always equal improvement.

The review step is the act of discussing the experience as a group or team immediately following the incident or activity, whenever possible. This process aids in producing continuous incremental improvement and in the discoveries of best practices. This is where the profit is found for any individual, team, or organization willing to follow this simple process by making it their own.

When operations, initiatives, or campaigns go wrong, it is usually fairly evident. It is at times like these when many who were involved in such mishaps or calamities become excited and begin to criticize the actions already executed or pile on suggestions of what can be done better the next time. But what usually happens when you succeed by meeting or exceeding your expectations? Do you pat each other on the back, or maybe you hit the bar at the end of the day for a few congratulatory drinks? With your current business procedures, how often do you and your teams take the time to figure out why success was achieved? A Class 1 Culture expects everything to be reviewed, even when things go well. And when necessary, revise with needed improvements to policies, procedures, processes, or future actions.

### 🔥 Hot Tip

$R^2$ provides for continuous individual, team, and organizational improvement.

In the previously described shopping mall fire, it was at this review where I truly appreciated how the $R^2$ process creates continuous individual, team, and organizational improvement—even my own.

As the leader of this group, I started the review to set the tone. This review meeting is not meant to be long and drawn out; rather, it is a short discussion to understand as much as possible about what occurred during the incident. If more time is needed because something critical is uncovered, then a specific meeting with all of the stakeholders would be scheduled. This meeting would provide a more in-depth review that would possibly lead to developing a list of issues, items, or procedures that need to be addressed in the revise process. This does happen when necessary, but it is not the norm.

The rules for a review are as follows: no egos, be honest with yourself, and remember the just culture that allows people to admit mistakes without fear of punishment, to learn from past mistakes and prevent future mistakes. This was my opportunity to provide a little coaching for my first-level leaders, the captains, and I began with a sincere thank-you for all of the efforts contributed by everyone involved. I discussed all of the positive things that I had observed and then asked these commanders to share my sincere appreciation with their teams for a job well done.

Overall, I was very pleased with how the operations were conducted in attacking and quickly extinguishing this fast-moving fire. I pointed out a couple of details regarding my actions that I could have done better, although nothing major, and I gave a quick overview of how I decided upon the strategy and tactics employed. Subsequent to my brief opening, we continued around the circle of captains and chiefs, each sharing experiences that included any tasks or actions that his or her teams performed: what went right, what went wrong, and why.

As usual, most of the needed improvements that were identified came from the team leaders themselves and pertained to the need for additional training for an individual or a firefighting team. The *revise* process for these training issues would be handled by the first-level supervisors, usually the captains.

At one point, one of the captains began reporting on his team's operations, and I couldn't believe what I was hearing. *Wait a minute*, I thought. *This captain is telling me that his crew extinguished the fire in the main fire area?* I had a recollection as to where every fire company was located and what their assigned tasks were during the firefighting operations, and this captain's report was challenging my recollection. I recalled that this captain and his crew had been assigned to a neighboring store to check for and, if necessary, prevent the spread of the fire into that store.

My staff assistant checked his written record. He found that the record did match what I thought had occurred. As we discussed this further, another captain spoke up and stated that he and his crew had been assigned to fire-attack duties but ended up in the store next to the main fire and wasn't where he had been assigned either. Both captains, during firefighting operations, did not realize that they were in the wrong place at that time. Only after the fire was extinguished and the smoke cleared out was it apparent to them that they had not been working where they thought they were.

None of this made any difference to the outcome of the firefighting efforts. The fire was extinguished, because firefighters get the right things done when needed. They got things done with a will-do attitude, even if they weren't exactly where they had been assigned.

You have probably heard of the fog of war, where soldiers get confused due to an overload of noise, distractions, and sometimes fear. Well, there's a similar phenomenon in firefighting with intense noise, lack of visibility, broken radio messages, and moments of fear. These sorts of things do happen.

This review serves to teach everyone present to be vigilant and prepared in the future for the issues, details, and other discoveries being discussed, as these challenges will always exist. What this review had uncovered is the fact that I had two firefighting teams working in a hazardous area, and I was not aware of their exact locations. If either team had put out a call for help, I wouldn't have had the correct location to dispatch the rescuers to their actual locations. In this case, the rescuers would be a team of firefighters that are standing by and ready to respond to the call "firefighter down."

As the incident commander, I was ultimately accountable for everything that happened during the firefighting operations. One of my many responsibilities is to know the exact whereabouts of each firefighting team—at all times. This review uncovered more information than I expected. I knew that my staff assistant and I would be revising our command post procedures to reduce the chance that this type of mix-up would happen in the future. I would also share any recommended changes to our process with my fellow battalion chiefs and their staff.

Employing a process like $R^2$ provides the opportunity to create success from failure and to ensure that successes are repeated as best practices. In this experience, we were lucky that no one was injured, lost, or killed. And the value was in learning of an issue that might have gone unnoticed. I was able to revise my process to improve future outcomes.

But, without this review, the improvement needed would have gone undiscovered. If the potential dangers were allowed to continue, at some point in time, they would have resulted in disaster. Instead, the result was a change in how I tracked and maintained control of teams that are under my command, improving operations and safety.

This incident illustrates how individuals, teams, and entire organizations can improve incrementally by taking the time to discuss completed activities. Your group will be able to turn their failures into future successes and to ensure that their successes are repeated as best practices.

## *Revise* Is Your Call to Action

Most of the issues discovered during the review can be corrected by the first-level leadership for individual- and team-performance improvement, using the revise step as a guide. But it is not enough to merely discover a failure or a success. The benefits of $R^2$ come from the fact that it is our call to action. The essence of the revise step: Once we discover that changes or improvements need to be made, we do something about it.

I was near the end of my firefighting career, and after 25 years of successfully utilizing the management, leadership, and success principles found in CPR for Business Success, the $R^2$ process was still able to improve my performance.

### 🔥 Hot Tip

$R^2$ ensures that the newest members of your team learn so much faster with a culture that expects a review of everything they do.

Following the review, the revise step can positively impact strategy, tactical operations, training, fire-prevention codes, or whatever is found that needs to be improved upon. In addition, when a newly discovered component of any activity proves extremely effective, it can be shared with the entire organization. This includes subsequent steps that document the discovery of newly found best practices, leading to the development of new or improved SOPs.

For the business world, the $R^2$ process will also translate into continuous incremental improvements for individuals, teams, and entire organizations. The newest members of your team will learn much faster within a culture that expects a review of everything they finalize. Everyone will learn, not only from his or her own experiences but also from the input of the more experienced employees. Senior associates will have a great deal of additional knowledge and experience, including successes and failures, to share with their less experienced colleagues.

Some of the best lessons that we have learned in both firefighting and in business were from observing others as they failed. It was usually fairly easy to see, as the poor results would speak for themselves; lessons were learned. But when we worked with people who were always doing things well—always succeeding—it wasn't as obvious to see why. Sometimes when people are performing at extraordinary levels, they make it look easy. This is because the hard work that occurs behind the scenes isn't always known to casual observers.

$R^2$ provides the proper perspective on what it takes to succeed in everything we do. This process allows individuals and teams to continuously improve by learning precisely what the more experienced team members are doing and how they make it look so easy.

Just like with firefighting teams, most of the issues or procedural problems you may discover during the review can be handled by first-level leadership, utilizing the revise process to address individual- or team-performance deficiencies. On a few occasions, there will be discoveries of opportunities for breakthrough improvements for your entire organization. This could include the development of new products, procedures, policies, and training programs. By following this process, you will decrease the time required to develop effective teams.

## Team Building: One Meeting at a Time

The $R^2$ process not only ensures continuous individual, team, and organizational improvement but also has the benefit of being a great team builder. Team members have the opportunity to understand and appreciate the responsibilities, challenges, and hard work of fellow team members. Everyone, at every level and in every position, will understand the importance of his or her actions and the actions of colleagues. It becomes very apparent how all of these actions contribute to the team's overall success.

A typical pushback from business leaders for this type of scheduled meeting is the following: "Our people have meeting fatigue, and the last thing we need is another reason for a meeting!" If your typical meetings are long and don't usually end up being of value to those in attendance, I would have to agree with the fatigue perspective. However, if you infuse your organization's culture with this process to quickly review everything a team has completed, a great deal of those other meetings will no longer be necessary. Look at it this way: If your culture allows for continuous incremental improvement for all by reviewing actions on an ongoing basis, then you can expect everyone to respond to a situation without having to call a meeting to discuss their future actions. This is because your review-and-revise meetings are actively preparing your teams to work better together in the future.

Remember this: When the flames are burning, firefighters don't usually have time for a meeting. It's typically after the fire is out where we discover what went right, what went wrong, and why.

---

**🔥 Hot Tip**

$R^2$ not only discovers what didn't work and why but also the secret to your success.

---

The $R^2$ process also provides a great opportunity to show appreciation for will-do efforts and assists in identifying where additional training may be needed. When all team members expect to be involved with a review of all actions, successful or otherwise, this process tends to encourage taking ownership for their efforts. Most people want to feel good about what they do, and most people will feel more motivated when they know their work is appreciated. Plus, everyone will become aware of the impact that each individual has on the team's performance.

Additionally, most people will work a little harder when they know that someone is paying attention to what they do. This is especially true when it's our peers and our leaders that are involved with the process. The $R^2$ process offers tremendous opportunities to publicly demonstrate appreciation for the hard work and effort that directly contributed to a successful outcome. These are the same types of successful outcomes that you want to replicate throughout your organization, as a cultural expectation, through inspirational leadership.

## Improve Your Customer Service for Dramatic Results

Another great use for $R^2$ is to ask your customers to provide input. Let them review how well they think you performed or if they believe something could have been improved upon. What better way than to use a process like $R^2$ to provide your customers with will-do service?

In business, I have used $R^2$ to win over clients and to develop new business opportunities. As a director for an air medical transport company, I would meet with hospital and emergency medical service supervisors to review patient-transport flights completed by one of my flight crews. If everything had gone well, it was a great opportunity to make the point that our commitment is for every flight to have the same trouble-free outcome.

If, on the other hand, there was a problem or complaint regarding our service, I would ask questions and then listen very carefully to the answers, while also taking notes. I would ask, "What went right, and why?" I followed this up by asking, "What went wrong, and why?" Most of the negative issues could be handled by me, the first-level business leader for the flight teams. There were also times when I discovered issues that needed to be corrected throughout our organization. I felt my call to action, so I would share these concerns with the appropriate individuals to make such changes and subsequent improvements.

On other occasions, I discovered something that worked so well that I would use the revise step as my call to action again, but then it was to share a suggestion for a major improvement to be replicated throughout the organization as a best practice. Even though these suggestions weren't always met with approval, the process typically allows for continuously being on the lookout for best practices and innovations.

Sharing the $R^2$ method with my clients worked wonders in building strong, trusting business relationships. I was able to be more responsive to their complaints and needs as I corrected operational deficiencies quickly. This put me in a position to always let my clients know that their input was appreciated.

Another way that I used the $R^2$ process in business worked like this: Every Monday, I would hold a leadership lunch meeting to review the week that had just passed. We would go around the table, much like the group of captains and battalion chiefs did while reviewing the fire, and each person would share what that person thought about the various tasks and initiatives that he or she was involved with during the previous week. We followed the same procedure—answering what went right, wrong, and why—followed with a consensus vote as to which issues should result in revising any of our policies, procedures, or processes. Having a weekly lunch with my leadership team while following the $R^2$ process has proven extremely beneficial for making incremental improvements and discovering best practices in teamwork, customer service, and risk management.

This review-and-revise process will provide positive results in your organization's culture. It will improve all aspects of accountability, best practices, communications, customer service, motivation, morale, productivity, teamwork, and work ethic. The resulting impact of this will be realized in your delivery of customer service. It will be noticeable.

Firefighters use this process to continually improve their effectiveness at saving the lives of their customers—that's a dramatic improvement. What would be a dramatic improvement for your customer service?

## Managing Risk While Discovering Your Best Practices

Risk management is a process that usually takes on many forms, depending on the industry and the complexity of the organization. The fire service is all about managing risk. This is because there is a great deal of risk, not only for firefighters but also for the general public to which the fire service has a duty and each firefighter has sworn an oath to protect.

There are inherent risks associated with firefighting and rescue operations. These risks are mitigated through the use of policies, training programs, and standard operating procedures (SOPs). There are also significant risks that are only acceptable when a decision has been made that the potential gain outweighs the risk and potential loss. The risk versus gain mind-set should be a routine thought process for all, especially for those in leadership positions.

The $R^2$ process has the ability to reinforce what is an acceptable level of risk and what is unacceptable. During the $R^2$ meeting that I conducted following the shopping mall fire, I identified an unacceptable risk: firefighting teams working in hazardous locations that are unknown to the incident commander. By reinforcing to the group of company commanders that this was dangerous and unacceptable, I was engaged in risk management. By improving my own command-post process for maintaining control of each firefighting teams' location, I was again engaged in risk management.

Risk management is at work throughout the review-and-revise process. Our ultimate goal is to discover not only what went wrong but also what went right. This is how we will continuously discover best practices that can lead to improved SOPs that will safely guide future actions. This is a critically important daily process for managing risk.

Whether you are leading firefighters fighting a fire or your own business "firefighters" engaged in the important work that brings success to your organization, risk management is probably part of your routine. If you desire to have consistent performance and reliable outcomes while also managing risk, then incorporating a process like $R^2$ is your call to action. Answering this call will provide your organization with a continuous stream of best practices, effective SOPs, and a safer work environment for all.

## $R^2$ = Exponential Improvement

You might be wondering why $R^2$ is used to illustrate the review-and-revise process. It is more than just a clever (or not-so-clever) approach to saying more with less. Utilizing this process is a powerful organizational culture enhancement because the benefits of improving the discovery and implementation of best practices, innovations, risk management, team building, and customer service are continuous. Consider the following explanation.

### First, think of the review step:

- Review all completed tasks.
- Two people reviewing one experience, or $2 \times 1 = 2$ opportunities to improve.
- Add a zero to demonstrate a larger workforce, and you have 20 people × 10 experiences = 200 opportunities to improve.

### Second, think of the revise step:

- Revise = a call to action.
- Two people each improving one future outcome, or $2 \times 1 = 2$ improved outcomes.
- Add a zero to demonstrate a larger workforce, and you have 20 people each improving their next 10 outcomes, or $20 \times 10 = 200$ improved outcomes.

The above explanation demonstrates how the $R^2$ process will exponentially improve individual, team, and organizational performance. In addition, all of the other benefits described will be experienced exponentially, delivering the power of continuous improvement and the discovery of best practices.

### Rules for Reviewing Your Team to Success:

When participating in the review, it is important for the leader to remind all participants of the rules:

1. No egos.
2. Be honest with yourself, and present an accurate account of actions.
3. Adopt the just culture.

The leader should begin with a review of his or her actions and experiences, setting an example in accordance with the stated rules. This action will set the tone for the $R^2$ process.

## The Review Process

Keep it simple, and keep it moving along, being certain that the following questions are answered by the group in regard to the tasks, procedures, and actions completed (refer to Figure 3.1).

1. What went right and what went wrong?
2. Why?
3. Identify issues, items, or procedures that need to be addressed in the revise process.

**Revise Process: This is the call to action.**

1. What will we do differently or better next time?
2. What is the size and scope of how we propose to improve?
3. Develop an action plan to improve future outcomes.

This two-step, review/revise process is intentionally simple to make it user friendly and to ensure that your teams are enthused about the benefits and that they look forward to the opportunity to participate.

Countless lives, both civilian and firefighter, have been saved through the culture that expects everything to be reviewed and, when necessary, revised. When organizations get behind a process like $R^2$, they will see positive results.

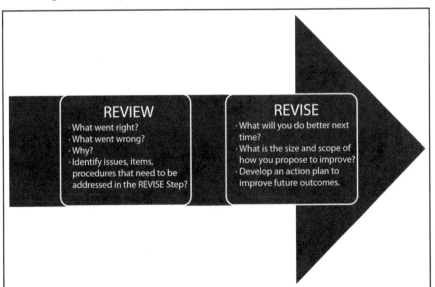

**FIGURE 3.1**

What will continuous incremental improvement do for you, your team, and your organization?

## Make Success a Way of Thinking—A Way of Life

Think back to chapter 2 and the power of thought that CPR for Business Success provides. Now, consider what might be possible in your professional and personal world if everyone consistently took command of everything he or she did by having a vision to solve problems, having effective planning skills, and responding to those plans with a focused will-do attitude. The only way to improve such an environment would be to add a step that insures everyone is continuously improving, discovering best practices and better customer service as well as building stronger teams, all while managing risk. This is the formula for success in everything you do:

## $CPR + R^2 = Success$

The fire service can't run a successful firefighting operation by remote control, and your organization can't run successfully by remote control either. This success formula is one of the many firefighting principles we have adapted for business that will improve your process, empower your people, and transform your culture (refer to Figure 3.2).

Utilizing the formula $CPR + R^2$ creates a cultural transformation. For many companies and organizations, the error rate continues to grow because they don't provide their people with processes that work, and then they fail

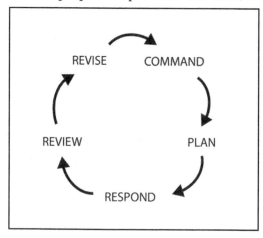

**FIGURE 3.2**

to examine the results of their actions. If you change your thoughts, you can change your culture. With this formula, achieving what you want becomes the predominant approach to your thinking. Once success becomes the way of thinking, it has already become the way of life.

Bird utilized this success formula in business, and this is what Gary Worth, CEO of St. Ives Laboratories Inc. had to say about his performance during his tenure with his corporation:

> Jim demonstrated unparalleled innovation in developing systems that continuously improved various operations in our business industry. His leadership contributed in discovering new methods for risk-management, analyses of problems and developing solutions that were instrumental in many of our company's successes. His contributions were directly responsible for annual extraordinary increases in incremental revenue and profits.

This process has been proven in business, and it can work in your business as well. Because the greatest assets you have are your human assets—which are also your greatest costs—doesn't it make sense to build a culture that has the ability to improve how your people perform? With this thought process, you can couple success to whatever you want to achieve: leadership success, organizational-culture success, career success, sales success, client relations success, and so forth.

What will your people experience with principles as simple as command, plan, respond, review, and revise? They will own a continuous thought process that acts like a mental checklist for critical thinking plus the expectation to continuously improve with a personal call to action and to serve the greater organization by sharing breakthrough discoveries. They will possess a class 1 way of thinking, the only way to build the Class 1 Culture.

## Chapter Review: Improve Your Process

Continuous incremental improvements for all and the discoveries of best practices are the premium values that are achieved by adding $R^2$ to your management and leadership processes. The challenge is to make it your own every day.

There are a great many benefits to following the $R^2$ process, and it works best when used as a formula that helps build a class-one way of thinking:

$CPR + R^2 = $ success.

$R^2$ is the review-and-revise process. Use it for continuous individual, team, and organizational improvement. When you do, the following benefits will result:

1. Accelerate the newest employees' learning by having them review as many of their significant actions as possible.
2. Drive innovation, inspire creativity, and publicize the unilateral contributions of the entire workforce.
3. Create a culture that embraces innovation and evolutionary change.
4. Transform your organizational culture to positively impact how people think about what they do and why they do it.
5. Improve your organization by discovering best practices that will keep you ahead of your competition.
6. Learn from your mistakes, reduce the number of mistakes, and turn failures into future successes.
7. Discover not only what didn't work and why but also the secrets to your successes.

$R^2$ doesn't only improve individual, team, and organizational performance; it also has a benefit of improving your efforts in team building, customer service, and risk management. You will be able to ensure that the things that work will be repeated, and the things that don't, won't.

What will continuous improvement do for you, your team, and your organization?

## Revise: This Is Your Call to Action

1. What will you do differently in your work and in your life?
2. What is the size and scope of how you propose to improve?

## Part Two

# Empower Your People

In part 1, we covered process-improvement principles. In part 2, we will explore principles that are aimed at empowering your leadership and your workforce. When process issues are not found to be the cause of poor performance, the next thing to do is to look at whether our people have the empowerment to be successful. Empowering our human resources takes leadership and organizational culture coming together to provide the support and guidance necessary to succeed.

When problems arise in any organization, the causes are usually either a process issue or a people issue. Because firefighting and rescue work are labor intensive, the fire service puts a great deal of focus on inspiring individual attitudes in order to empower the workforce as a whole to get the right things done for the right reason.

- In chapter 4, we cover the critical ingredients needed for high-performance teamwork.
- In chapter 5, we look at crisis management and how to be prepared to deal with any crisis that you and your team may face, together.
- In chapter 6, we explain a simple system you can use to tune out the noise in your life, start to set goals, and develop an uncontrollable desire to turn your goals into reality.

# You Go . . . I Go: Anatomy of High-Performance Teamwork

*The secret of success is consistency of purpose.*

—Benjamin Disraeli

From our first day in the fire academy and throughout our nearly 50 years of combined firefighting experience, there is one tenet that stands out as the greatest cultural advantage that defines what the fire service is all about: teamwork. The fire service culture requires firefighters to work together at all times. Think about what it means if someone says, "You go . . . I go!" For the fire service, it means that we do better when we work together, and it is a cultural imperative for safety and success. Everyone within your organization will also do better by working together with the same type of teamwork. This chapter is dedicated to providing the essential ingredients necessary to produce high-performance teamwork in any organization or profession.

On May 4, 1988, at 10:37 p.m., the Los Angeles City Fire Department's dispatch center received a 911 call reporting a fire in the tallest high-rise building in the city, the 62-story First Interstate Bank Building. The first fire chief to arrive reported to the emergency dispatch center that there was fire showing from most of the windows on the 12th floor. Taking command of the firefighting and rescue operations, he requested a large number of additional resources that would eventually have nearly half of the on-duty firefighters from the LAFD's 103 fire stations working together to save lives and protect property.

Among the additional responding firefighting resources were firefighting helicopters with "airborne engine companies" onboard.[1] These airborne firefighting teams were amongst the first of their kind, with each member being specially trained to respond onboard a helicopter to emergencies that required capabilities considered beyond the reach of ordinary fire and rescue resources.

The City of Los Angeles operates its own fire department Air Operations Section, typically referred to as "Air Ops." The fire personnel assigned to this section operate four medium-lift helicopters and two smaller helicopters for observation and command functions. At the time of this fire, the section also included hoist rescue teams specially trained for rescuing people stranded in locations where a helicopter could not safely land. The Air Ops teams were designed to go wherever their firefighting and rescue skills were needed. On this night, they were needed on the roof of the 62-story office building that would soon have floors 12 through 16 fully ablaze.

The initial communications with the building's security personnel included an urgent message: Approximately 40 people who had been working as part of a nightly cleaning crew were unaccounted for and possibly trapped on upper floors. These airborne engine firefighting teams were being flown to the roof of the towering structure with one main goal: enter the smoke- and heat-filled stairwell and make their way down into the burning building to search for the trapped workers.

During this airborne deployment, one of the observation helicopter pilots spotted a man on the 50th floor. The pilot reported that the man was at the window, waving a curtain in an attempt at getting his attention. With a confirmed victim's location, a plan was immediately developed by the Air Ops team's leaders to launch a rescue. The decision was made to send in several two-person search-and-rescue teams with specific floor assignments. Their goal was to rescue the man in the window as well as any other trapped occupants along the way.

For over an hour, periodically engulfed in the relentless smoke, the pilot continued the dangerous and skillful maneuver, hovering the helicopter alongside the 860-foot-tall structure. The pilot was utilizing the aircraft's high-powered spotlight to maintain a visual of the exhausted and faltering man at the window; the smoke inside the building was obviously taking its toll on the victim's ability to breathe.

Other firefighters climbing the stairs from street level successfully met the challenges of the heat, smoke, and extreme physical and mental fatigue as they also made their way up to the 50th floor. By the time firefighters reached the man in the window, he was unconscious. Doing whatever they could to try to save the man's life, the airborne engine company firefighters teamed up with the other firefighters who had climbed the stairs from the ground level. As they constantly administered oxygen to the man, firefighters took turns carrying him up the final 12 floors. Together, they all made their way up the dark, smoke-filled stairwell to the roof. The victim was loaded onto a helicopter and flown to a trauma center, where he eventually recovered from his horrific experience.

Throughout the evening, while the Air Ops teams responded to the plan to save people trapped on floors above the inferno, hundreds of other firefighters working in teams were equally confronted with the heat, smoke, and physical exhaustion that comes with any high-rise firefighting operation. Before it was over, this emergency had become the largest and most difficult high-rise firefighting operation ever waged by the LAFD.

The firefighters, paramedics, helicopter pilots, airborne rescue teams, law enforcement officers, and others, working in difficult and dangerous conditions, saved this man's life. Simultaneously, there was an array of other teams at this major emergency, performing many other equally dangerous tasks involved with fighting the fire on multiple floors. All the while, other firefighters continued searching the smoky darkness in search of anyone who might still be trapped.

During the review of this fire, it was determined that the helicopters were critical to the success and the mitigation of multiple facets of the overall emergency incident. It was also noted that, had this fire broken out during normal business hours with hundreds of people on the roof needing to be evacuated, these airborne teams could have performed a tremendous number of rescues. By utilizing the same management and leadership principles found in "CPR for Business Success," these teams had demonstrated their effectiveness and ability to take command of the situation, size up a plan, and repeatedly respond to the plan with a focused will-do attitude.

The entire firefighting effort demonstrated what high-performance teams are capable of accomplishing, even in the most extraordinary situations. At that time, the situation confronted by the air operation teams was, in some ways, uncharted territory. This was a testament to the eclectic skills and courage of each team member, and more to the theme of this chapter, it was a case in point on the anatomy of high-performance teamwork.

## Creating a High-Performance Team

If you think back to chapter 1 and how the fire academy training officers are tasked with turning a group of ordinary people into a team that is inspired and motivated to respond to extraordinary situations, generally speaking, the fire service represents a high-performance team. This high-rise fire is a great example of the need for any organization to nurture a culture that knows how to focus on success. Additionally, it points to the need for individuals within the organization to believe that what they do is important, and why they do it always matters to someone.

Most people have either been part of or have observed a low-performance team environment. Each situation is most likely somewhat unique, but overall, most of the poorly performing teams that we have witnessed had two things in common: poor leadership and a negative, low-expectation culture. Low performance seems like a very easy thing to accomplish. If someone wanted to set out to create low-performance teamwork, all that person would need to do is ensure that the people in supervisory positions had no idea how to positively influence the behavior of others, while also ensuring that the culture was ingrained with a negative feeling about anything and everything. But because we want to focus on the things that will build the right organizational culture and leadership, we will focus on how to succeed at team building.

To build a high-performance team in any organization requires the same type of principles of leadership and culture found in the fire service. The reason we should all desire high-performance teamwork is so that we have the confidence that our people are capable of performing at their best and that their motivation comes from knowing what needs to be done to achieve success.

What if leaders of business teams practiced fire service principles to experience extraordinary outcomes within their respective industry or profession? Other than the actual work environment, the main difference between firefighting and business is perspective. Wherever people are involved, the same principles of leadership and culture apply. Leaders in any environment—who are wise and knowledgeable in their field—will keep their eyes on the big things while ensuring that the small things are also being accomplished. They will skillfully communicate their vision along with their plans to achieve that vision. To provide a great deal of certainty and confidence amongst a leadership team and a workforce, organizational stability is maintained with a focus on success.

If you follow this thinking, you will be on your way to building the teams that will provide the outcomes you are looking for. To review how group dynamics play an important part in the development of a high-performance team, let's start with the basics. The very basic needs for ordinary teamwork are:

## People + Desire + Trusted Leadership = Teamwork

To realize high-performance teamwork that can and will respond to extraordinary situations with a high level of success requires more than the ordinary. High-performance teamwork requires components like trusted inspirational leadership and a culture that rewards people for expanding their comfort zones by taking acceptable risks that make sense. People will only take risks if there is trust and confidence between team members and, more importantly, between the rank-and-file members and their leaders.

Consistency is one of the major qualities on which team members can build trust in each other and in their leaders. Building trust in leadership strengthens the confidence of the team members. Trusted leaders must be consistent in order for their teams to be able to anticipate how their leaders will react in different situations. Feeling the confidence that comes from the consistency of purpose is one of the ways that team members will believe that they can trust in their leaders.

Beyond the needed consistency of leadership, all involved must also be acutely aware of the expectations for every member of the team. This will allow group dynamics to create an inner strength that comes from a shared purpose, or mission. These dynamics have the power to morph into teamwork. Trusted teamwork eventually sows mutual respect. No team member, or anyone else for that matter, wants to fail or to disappoint anyone with whom he or she shares mutual respect; mutual respect is the cornerstone for any high-performance team.

Effective teams must include different personalities and skill sets that can operate collectively. For the Air Ops teams, for example, these included helicopter pilots, paramedics, firefighters, engineers, and captains. Each individual contributed a specific skill set that allowed these teams to be focused on the success of their assigned goals. Individually, no single team member has all the answers, but together, the well-balanced team can find the answers to deliver success.

Any high-performance team must have the right combination of individuals necessary to achieve the desired goals for the specific environment.

Even though we believe that most people are ordinary people, we also believe that ordinary people are capable of some pretty extraordinary things. The right combination of ordinary people can, with the right culture and leadership, achieve extraordinary successes.

We're not talking about bringing together perfect people. Firefighters are certainly not without typical human flaws, just like the people who work in any profession. Everyone doesn't need to hang out together during time off, but if they do, it's all the better. The critical requirement is that everyone shares a common purpose that promotes professional and personal bonds. The resulting team camaraderie is one of the key ingredients that causes firefighters to risk it all to help a fellow firefighter. This is also why firefighters are willing to expose themselves to high levels of personal danger to save the lives of total strangers. They feel a sense of empowerment because they know that their teammates will go the distance to rescue them if necessary. Do the people in your organization have a feeling of support from one another and from their leaders that provides the same sense of empowerment?

A high-performance team starts with the very culture needed for it to exist, a culture of consistent and common purpose. The foundation and influence for the life of that culture must come from the top levels of the organization. It won't "bubble up" from the bottom ranks to spread throughout the organization. To have a lasting effect on the organization, it must come from the highest levels of leadership and be exemplified by all levels of leadership.

Having a common purpose and a strong desire to achieve success is how firefighters build high-performance teams that can work successfully in high-stress and potentially deadly work environments. Fire service leaders set the tone for such outcomes by building a culture that is dedicated to a mission, vision, and values that must be a way of thinking shared by all.

As covered in chapter 1, a meticulously thought-out and well-worded mission statement unites by providing the right common purpose for your organization. Having a strong vision statement creates synergy by revealing a desired future state, defining success, and empowering all members with the knowledge of how they can contribute. And specific values that are deemed important for the team's, company's, or organization's success must be defined and accepted by everyone involved.

Let's take a closer look at each of these vital building blocks of a high-performance team: mission, vision, and values.

## Mission to Motivation

In chapter 1, we discussed how important a properly worded mission state-ment is to any organization, because it provides each individual with a foun-dation for thought and action, especially during difficult challenges. We can't have a discussion about the anatomy of high-performance teamwork without again touching on the importance of mission—it's that significant.

After leaving the fire service, I took some time to go on a vacation with my wife, in Italy. We were taking in the sights of an old church as we started up a narrow stone stairway. We were climbing the stairs to the top of the dome, when I suddenly started to feel claustrophobic. I made it up a cou-ple more levels in the enclosed stairwell, and then I just had to get out. I turned around and abruptly announced to my wife that I needed to go back outside.

As I quickly headed out, she got concerned and followed me down the stairs. Once we were outdoors, she asked, "What was that all about?"

I told her that I wasn't sure where we were going or what we were going to see when we got there. For some reason, the walls of that narrow stairway seemed to start closing in on me, and, well, I just had to get out.

I noticed her facial expression was one of disbelief as she said, sounding a bit confused, "But you were a firefighter for 25 years! How could you have done all the things you had to do if you're claustrophobic?"

I thought that she had a very good point, so I pondered it for a moment. What I discovered is that if I had been in the same situation, but I was told that someone needed my help at the top of the narrow, enclosed stairs, I wouldn't have given it a second thought. I would have had a mission to help someone. I would have taken command of the situation and completed a quick size-up, and then I'd be on my way. I would not have cared how nar-row or how far those stairs would go.

I had just discovered how to explain the importance of serving a mis-sion: It is inspiring and motivating. Having a mission can keep everyone focused on the immediate task at hand, while also preventing all of the excessive noise and distractions, like a sudden bout with claustrophobia, from becoming barriers to getting things done.

Having a mission motivates people by telling them why it's important to go where they must go, even if they don't really want to go there. When two or more people come together, accountable for the same mission state-ment, the resulting synergy makes difficult things seem easier, the impos-sible seem possible, and any encountered pain more bearable.

Imagine that you're sleeping in a dormitory with other firefighters. Suddenly, the lights pop on, the alarm tones sound, and a dispatcher's voice blares from the ceiling speaker telling you what the problem is, who is to respond, and the location where they must go. If waking at home to your alarm at 3:00 a.m. is painful, imagine doing it for the third or fourth time after midnight. Yet, it doesn't actually seem so painful in a room full of people having a shared motivation to move in the same direction with a common purpose. For firefighters, relying on this common purpose to deal with the pain of exhaustion is truly a game changer. In fact, fire stations that experience high call loads, with many emergency calls coming in during the nighttime hours, are known as houses of pain. This is because firefighters work hard all day, and when they finally hit the beds late at night, they are physically worn out. Any parents who have brought home a newborn baby know that feeling of exhaustion; just as they are drifting off to sweet, precious sleep, they are abruptly awakened by the cry of the baby. You love the job or the baby, but it's still painful.

Once you have developed teamwork within a group, synergy is born. But it is the mission that creates motivation, an essential ingredient in high-performance teamwork. High-performance teams must have a common purpose to experience the motivation to achieve shared success. When team members share a duty to serve a stated mission and respond in like fashion, they create motivation in each other. One of the greatest elements of a well-written mission statement is that every person on your team will use it as the same foundation for decision making. Regardless of his or her specific responsibilities or status on the team or in the organization, everyone is motivated by the same mission but from a different perspective.

A clear and concise mission statement defines, in the simplest terms, your organization's core reason for being, and it had better not be all about money. Money is definitely important to most of society, and it is a motivator. But many people aspire to be part of something more meaningful than just a paycheck. They want a paycheck that is also connected to a culture that offers greater intrinsic values.

If all an organization offers its employees is a monetary incentive, many—especially the talented—will leave as soon as they find comparable income elsewhere. In general, this practice can create an organization with a hiring revolving door, attracting people who are motivated by money, only to lose them when the next bigger ticket can be punched by going through the next door. This type of organizational environment makes team building very difficult to accomplish.

Emphasizing a meaningful mission statement will help to create the inner strength of confidence for, and within, each individual. This feeling of confidence throughout the group turns into high-performance teamwork. The right mission statement will infuse your organization with the collective commitment necessary for business success. It can also have a positive impact on innovative thinking, possibly inspiring new business ideas that fit the mission of the organization.

For example, the fire service successfully took on the delivery of emergency medical service (EMS) in the 1970s because it fit the mission statement of saving lives. Today, the majority of emergency calls that firefighters answer are in the delivery of EMS. Think about your organization's mission statement and how it might be the foundation for innovation. What new business opportunity might fit your organization's core purpose?

There is a very essential point to keep in mind about the importance of your organizational mission. Without a well-defined mission statement driving their motivation, your people will create their own agendas. This will cause them to respond to a given situation in a manner each person deems to be appropriate. When this happens, you no longer have a team, but rather a group of people all acting independently of one another—in a word, chaos.

During the high-rise fire, if each of the Air Ops team members had his or her personal agenda, there is no way the team could have succeeded at saving lives that night. For example, let's imagine that the helicopter pilots had not felt the need to take on the risky and stressful maneuver of providing an aircraft on the smoke-shrouded roof or hovering alongside the building. It was because of their mission that they willfully accepted these challenges. Whether maintaining a visual on the man clinging to life at the window or being available to immediately evacuate firefighters and fire victims whenever they happened to appear from the penthouse stairwell, the right mission was driving team motivations.

A meaningful, succinct, success-focused mission statement must be clear and concise. Just as the fire service mission of "saving lives and protecting property" is definitely to the point, so too should all mission statements be that are meant to drive successful decision making. If it is your intention that your people live it and use it, "it" must be easy to remember. Every member of your organization must understand what the mission means to them, and it should have a statement with which they are proud to be associated.

The successful mission statement is a tool that all leaders of any size of company or organization should use to reach their goals. This is especially true when the leaders can't always be physically present with their followers. And depending on the work environment, that is probably most of the time. This is a meaningful step toward empowering your people to consistently get things done in a manner that serves your organization's core reason for being in business.

## From Vision to Reality

Like mission, chapter 1 also touched on vision, and again, we can't have a complete discussion about high-performance teamwork without including the importance of having a guiding vision.

Every member of a high-performance team must thoroughly understand the vision that the team leader has developed for the team. Each individual must accept his or her part in contributing to the realization of the vision. To accomplish this, a good place to start is to ensure that everyone knows and understands not only the vision but also the plan, the definition of success, and the goals in priority order. Simply put, make sure that you always know what you and your team are trying to do and why you and your team are trying to do it.

When the incident commander of the high-rise fire arrived on the scene, he had the benefit of a thought process like CPR for Business Success. As he rapidly became aware of the current situation and considered all of the resources at his disposal, he was also defining what success would look like for the eventual control of the overall emergency. This included the analysis of the many tasks needing to be accomplished and the subsequent prioritizing of goals. In doing so, he had just created his vision for the incident. As he completed his size-up, he was well aware that the plan he was developing was a type of road map as to how his vision for the abatement of this emergency would be realized.

With routinely scheduled preresponse planning sessions to simulate a high-rise fire and regular training on individual skills employed during this type of emergency situation, the leader's vision had already been communicated long before this particular fire ever started. This is because firefighters responding to this emergency had already trained for a high-rise firefighting plan. Their previous training and experiences contributed to their understanding of the goals for their potential assignments and for how the IC would likely define success.

🔥 **Hot Tip**

Your vision should be communicated in present-tense, powerful, and positive language to indicate a desired future reality. It is also important for leaders to maintain a fresh vision for everyone in the organization, company, department, or team. This can be accomplished by displaying it in printed materials and through verbal communications as well as actions.

Each firefighter developed a similar overall vision. And once that person received an assigned task, they would focus on their specific goals for that task. Each team member would also complete an individual size-up to provide situational awareness. These steps created a high level of confidence in what he or she was about to do, allowing that firefighter to respond with a will-do attitude. This is how firefighters are empowered to focus on success so that they can contribute to making the incident commander's vision a reality. Knowing and understanding this shared vision is the first step in helping to create such a future reality. Vision shows people where they must go. Vision is destination.

Whether it is creating a vision for the entire organization, a team within the organization, a business project such as a product launch, or a high-rise fire, a vision cannot lead to reality unless it is shared through continuous two-way communication. Leaders are most effective when they can influence the positive behaviors of others through different modes of communication. Creating a vision and repeating it often, in a clear and meaningful way, is a mandatory function for leaders of high-performance teams. A vision statement is an illustration of where your team is going. It is a desired future outcome that will become reality if everyone on the team knows it, believes it is possible, and discovers how they can contribute to making it a future reality.

## Values for All

On that May evening in 1988, at the moment the alarm sounded for each firefighting team involved, each and every firefighter immediately knew that what he or she was about to do was important. The firefighting teams didn't yet know about the man trapped on the 50th floor or the many others who needed to be rescued, not to mention the numerous businesses that could lose everything to the flames and smoke. What they did know was that performing their duties to the best of their abilities would matter to someone, because it always does. But how do business teams that don't routinely deal with life-or-death scenarios come to believe that what they do is important and that doing their best always matters to someone?

In any profession, a high-performance team will have a belief in each of its members. To achieve such a mutual feeling of respect, there must be a set of rules or standards that have to be adhered to. These standards or values define parameters for competency, communications, trust, accountability, consistency, and positive attitudes. They also work to prevent the disorder that comes from jealousy or selfish ambitions within the team. The right values create a culture that inspires everyone to do their best. This is vitally important to the entire team, not just to the individual, and it gets to the heart of what teamwork means.

Once a team or organization has created a list of values, these values must be accepted by every member of the team. These values, when coupled with mission and vision, build a culture that focuses on success and the will to do whatever it takes to achieve it. We refer to this as a Will-do attitude. This type of attitude is the only acceptable way for individuals on a team to think about what they will face together and, together, what they will do about it. If you look in the mirror and ask yourself, "Will I respond today as though it matters?" What would your answer be? Maintaining a will-do attitude is a requirement for high-performance team members. It allows them to consistently inspire each other to focus on success.

In addition to the team values, leaders need to facilitate a private discussion with each individual to discover how that person views his or her position within the team. The outcome of this exchange must be an intrinsic belief that what the person does is important and that doing it well always matters so someone. Ask, "Who does it matter to?" Just like the fire academy captains in chapter 1, inspirational leaders are able to help their followers put a face on who benefits when they succeed and who gets hurt when they don't. The answers aren't as important as the fact that each individual discovers these answers for themselves. When people personalize what they do and why they do it, they will be living the will-do attitude.

High-performance teams have the will-do attitude because it supports their belief that what they do always matters to someone. Because of this, they almost always find a way to work together. Compare this with someone who responds to a given task by saying, "I'll see if I can get to it." The right values will take your team from a slacker "I'll see" response to a high-performing "will-do" response.

**Hot Tip**

Meaningful mission, vision, and values statements give meaning to the principle of doing the right things for the right reasons and at the right time.

We have experienced in the business world situations wherein trusted leadership also creates a similar type of attitude. We have discovered business cultures that have inspired extraordinary efforts, innovations, and accomplishments by overtly recognizing these high-performance traits as professional pride. In these situations, it is almost without exception that these business organizations also possess a successful mission statement, vision statement, and list of values that are known to all of the company's associates.

The right mission, vision, and values are inspired by the right leadership principles that reach deep within an organization's culture. The importance of this cannot be understated, because there are times when every company or organization will experience a shock to its system. And whether it is a change in the marketplace, a change in leadership, a careless act, an act of war, or an act of God, challenging events happen to all of us. When an organization has taken the time to craft and implement these critical drivers of success, it will benefit from a culture that has momentum, and it will keep going in the desired direction despite experiencing extreme shocks.

The fire service has experienced shocks like this throughout its history. For example, during the Los Angeles riots of 1992, firefighters were deliberate targets of gunfire as they struggled to stay true to their mission to fight over 3,000 arson fires. The mission had not changed, but the strategy and tactics had to be adjusted to continue serving the same mission.

During and after the 9/11 terrorist attacks in New York, Washington, D.C., and Pennsylvania, the fire service received an incredible shock to the system of firefighting and rescue operations. The 343 firefighters who lost their lives at the World Trade Center willingly rushed into harm's way. They did it because their mission told them that it was the only way to save thousands of people—who were successfully evacuated—prior to the structural collapse of the World Trade Center towers. Even with the horrendous loss of life and the extreme physical pain and emotional anguish suffered by countless others, the mission continued with an understanding of the new challenges that all firefighters would face as they would continue to save lives and protect property with our nation at war.

Mission drives motivation; vision provides direction for each challenge; and values empower people to unite and respond to extraordinary situations. A Class 1 Culture must have these three foundational building blocks in place to prevent the extreme shocks from becoming dead ends, instead of mere speed bumps.

To create the mission, vision, and values that fit any organization requires a reevaluation to define and fully understand what the organization does and why the organization does it. To support and to guide those who follow such principles requires continuous involvement from all levels of trusted leadership. To propagate these principles throughout the organization, leaders must first take the time to develop their own meaningful mission, vision, and values. Once completed, they will have given meaning to the principle of doing the right things for the right reasons and at the right time.

## Leading with Appreciation, Trust, and Respect

The fire chiefs who took command of the various operational functions at the high-rise fire appreciated what the firefighters were enduring throughout this extremely challenging situation. They had walked and even crawled in these firefighters' boots before. They knew what it was like for everyone inside the burning hallways and offices high above their street level command post. Because of the past experiences and the competence of these leaders, the firefighters trusted in the strategies and tactics employed. The firefighters also respected the difficult decisions that their leaders had to make. And the respect went both ways, as the leaders were in awe of the tremendous effort expended under some of the most difficult firefighting conditions imaginable.

Try to imagine that you are climbing up the stairs to reach anywhere from 11 to 62 floors. You are wearing protective gear that adds approximately 60 pounds to your total weight, and you are also carrying another 50 to 60 pounds of hose or other equipment. You finally arrive at your assigned destination, exhausted. When you make entry onto your assigned floor, you endure extreme heat as you crawl on your belly to stay as low as possible, trying to escape the highest temperatures at the ceiling, possibly 2,000 degrees. As you make your way toward the fire, becoming entangled in a maze of debris that slows your forward progress, you discover that the carpet covering the floor you are crawling on is melting beneath you. As you work with your team, struggling to pull your hoseline into position, the smoke makes it impossible to see anything.

Suddenly, the red-orange glow of the flames is visible in a scene that resembles an image right out of Dante's *Inferno*. Within 15 minutes, the low-air alarm of at least one of your team members sounds, and it's time to withdraw and head down to a staging area, usually 2 floors below the lowest fire floor. Your team takes on refilled air cylinders and gets a drink of water, and you're off to do it all over again. This scenario will repeat until the fire is finally knocked down and the entire building has been thoroughly searched for anyone still inside.

Not one of these firefighters arrived at this major emergency unprepared to do their best. Think back to chapter 1, and remember how the fire academy began the process of enlarging each new firefighter's comfort zones. Do you remember how this led to discovering that ordinary performance wasn't good enough to achieve the truly important things and why trust was so important for building confidence in our leaders? This high-rise fire was the type of situation that could not have resulted with such extraordinary success without the culture and leadership that empowers people to go the distance—to get the hard things done and to go up and over.

As difficult as this description of high-rise firefighting seems, we only wanted to give you an example of why high-performance teamwork principles exist in the first place. Now, think about what you and your team must accomplish every day. Hopefully, your work environment doesn't look like Dante's *Inferno*, but the need to succeed is probably just as important.

It might even seem that with high-performance teamwork, the team would actually run itself. But the truth is, whenever two or more people come together to accomplish something, leadership is required.

There are teams that consist of highly technical individuals who have the will-do spirit. Each person is charged up and prepared at all times to take action. The leader of such a team must be able to harness the talents and enthusiasm of this type A group. He or she must be able to make good decisions that move the team harmoniously in the same direction to achieve shared goals. Utilizing the many principles covered here, leaders can greatly impact the team's culture through their decision-making process.

By using the same principles described here, Bird was very successful during his business career, with his decision-making skills standing out amongst other business leaders. This is how Richard J. Hynes, president of international business for Alberto Culver explained it:

> In a mode of cross-functional teaming Jim included operations, sales, marketing and finance with a bias for action and results, and a solid organizational understanding. Unique, and possibly due to his background as a firefighter, Jim always maintained perspective and was a voice of reason with the group. Problem solving seemed to come naturally!

With this example in mind, remember that before goals can be set and prioritized, leaders must first become skilled decision makers. The fire service adheres to a hybrid model of decision making known as consultative, which is a combination of command decision making and consensus decision making.

The consultative model, in all management fields, is utilized by leaders who solicit input from their subordinates or direct reports to consider such feedback before making decisions. Consultative decision making is valued in firefighting, where it is impossible to make the best decisions when there are other people on the team that possess more information than the leader. A prime example is the fire chief in command of the firefighting operations at the high-rise fire, who is positioned at the command post located outside of the burning building.

The incident commander is responsible for developing a plan that includes strategy and tactics to be put into action by the team members. He or she is the one person on whom ultimate accountability for the outcome of all operations rests. However, the IC's plan, developed solely from the command post's perspective, may not be the best solution. Input from the inside of the burning building where engaged firefighting captains are aware of—and directly affected by—real-time conditions is critical. The firefighting captain's input is appreciated by the IC because it allows him or her to see the situation through a set of trusted eyes.

Utilizing two-way communication with the inside captains provides the most current, and probably the most accurate, information that can be obtained. The IC can then adjust strategies and tactics and then assign tasks and directives to implement any change to the plan. Typically, effective two-way communications are maintained throughout the firefighting operation. It is vital to establish two-way communications immediately to make the best decisions based on the most current and accurate information. Once a decision is made, however, the decision is translated into assignments and directives that are clear and well communicated.

Without this type of consultative approach, many organizations can risk the development of blind obedience. Blind obedience is found in a low-performance culture of nonthinkers that do only what they are ordered to do, despite any negative consequences that might occur. In firefighting, this could be deadly, and in business—depending on what type—it could be just as lethal.

Once a decision for action is made, how can leaders ensure that their teams will follow? Leaders in all professions must earn trust and respect from their followers to become more influential. One way to accomplish this is to appeal to deeper motives than merely wages and benefits for accepting the challenging and critical work usually given to the high-performance team. Emphasizing with words and actions the cultural significance of mission, vision, and values helps to create inspiration, and it can go a long way in building trust and respect within the team.

But what about the times when a team gets off track and loses focus of what it is working toward—more specifically, when team members have forgotten their definition of success? When this occurs, it takes trusted leadership to take command of the situation by assisting the team in reestablishing its focus on the vision. This type of circumstance demonstrates the importance of trust. Trust in leadership strengthens when members believe that the leaders have their best interest in mind. If you make a slight adjustment in how you present the facts to your team members, they will be more inclined to heed your appeal to improve their actions and performances.

Trust will not come merely due to the promotion of a leader to a more elevated role or to a position of greater responsibility. Trust can only be developed over time. Teams watch, listen, and evaluate what a leader says and how he or she says it as well as the subsequent and corresponding actions of the leader. Teams will then make their assessments as to the trustworthiness of those in leadership positions. Trust is the most important part of leadership. Without trust, one can never be a successful leader.

In a business situation, I witnessed a layoff of ten employees due to financial challenges facing the company. All received little notice and were left unemployed just in time for the Thanksgiving holidays; it seemed ironic at the time. Their individual performances had been highly rated, with some being previously promoted, and some of their areas of responsibility had been touted as the model of best practices for the company. Each of these employees was offered a severance package in a range of a maximum three weeks of salary to nothing at all.

Was this an example of trust and respect for people? Or was this a declaration by the management team that people are merely things that are managed and can be discarded like other things that are managed? Only those involved would know for sure, but a major problem with the treatment of employees in this manner is the perception of those employees that remain with the company. All of them had been witness to the leadership, or lack thereof, demonstrated.

Leading by example does not guarantee success. If your example is dishonest, unethical, or unjust, people will respond with their feet by exiting when they get the chance. However, if you are the right example, your followers will remain loyal, trusted, and respectful employees who will continuously contribute to your brand, your culture, and your success. They will strive to be more like you.

Successful leaders respect the dedication, experience, talents, and importance of their employees. Leaders at all levels, with vision, are aware that all of their actions are noticed and evaluated by their team members, particularly those that are the most talented and productive workers. Exceptional leaders are seen by their team members as appreciative, trustworthy, and respectful.

Especially in difficult financial times, leadership must demonstrate appreciation, trust, and respect for all employees. Systems, processes, and procedures need to be managed. People, the most important resources that an organization has, need and crave trusted leadership that they respect. They appreciate it.

## Doing the Right Things for the Right Reasons

Trusted and respected leadership really boils down to doing the right things for the right reasons. The right culture for an organization makes this idea easier to understand. As we have driven home previously, you can demonstrate this way of thinking when you share an organizational mission that serves as a foundation for thought and for action. Add to that a vision that serves as the keystone that locks in the collective understanding of a common destination with the values to empower your people to connect the two.

As a battalion chief, I experienced a difficult situation that put me in a position where these cultural principles guided my thinking and my actions. I was in command of a fire that resulted in the death of a four-year-old boy. It was an experience that proved to me, once again, how important these cultural ingredients are. It also reinforced for me the importance of being grounded in principles like doing the right things for the right reasons.

The first responding companies were faced with one apartment unit fully involved with fire. As firefighters approached the doorway to make entry and attack the flames, frantic parents pleaded with them to save their young son who was still in his bedroom. It was immediately obvious that the boy's survival was impossible. The firefighters, nonetheless, continued to fight hard to knock down the blaze. Unfortunately, the boy had died in his bed prior to the arrival of the first responding firefighters.

**🔥 Hot Tip**

Doing the right things for the right reasons may not always be seen as the best business decision. It will, however, always produce results that you and your team can be proud of.

Due to this fatality, an arson investigation team responded to investigate the cause of the fire. Throughout the fire investigation, the firefighters, the boy's family, and the news media all anticipated the moment when the boy's body would be removed and placed into a coroner's vehicle in a dignified manner.

Anyone with a heart can imagine how difficult this day was for everyone involved. Emotions were written all over the faces of the firefighters as they remained strong and resilient while trying to comfort the family during this tragic time.

The news media had arrived and sought to interview me, the incident commander. I provided the basic known facts to their questions. The video crews were pressing me to get close-up shots of the fire scene. Due to the nature of the incident, with a fatality involved, I couldn't allow the news crew to approach beyond the sidewalk. We had the area blocked off with yellow tape with black letters that read: "Fire Line Do Not Pass." I had explained to the photographers and videographers that once the coroner was complete with his duties, I would allow them get their shots.

When the coroner began to make his exit of the building, one of the captains pulled me aside. He informed me that he discovered the coroner's body bag was semitranslucent, not the usual black. At this time, the boy's entire family had not been notified of his condition. It was our concern that the subsequent television broadcast, which would include the incident address and the see-through body bag, would make it fairly obvious to anyone watching the news coverage that the fatality was a small child. This would be devastating to any family members not yet aware of this tragedy and who might be learning about it watching the story on TV. This would obviously be a terrible way for a loved one to find out about the fate of this young boy.

The captain told me that his firefighters feared that the video crew would be able to get a video shot of them removing the deceased child from the apartment. They urged the captain to ask me if they could hold up a large tarp to protect the scene from the cameras. I agreed, and then I went to address the media—all still waiting for the shot.

As I walked up to an angry group of media professionals, some were saying things like, "Hey, Chief, you said we could get our shots!" and, "We have a right to information, and you can't suppress that information!"

My initial thought was to say something like the following: "You are all a bunch of vultures and need to get out of my face!" I did not say that, because I realized that there are times when leaders must put the needs of their position and their team first; I needed to use my emotions to inspire. I made a conscious decision to outwardly demonstrate a calm demeanor.

Holding back my emotions, I raised my arms and motioned to bring them all together. I said to the agitated members of the media, "Hey, guys, my intention was to allow you to get your shots. It turns out that the boy's entire family has not been notified and, for some reason, the coroner has used a see-through body bag! You all know that we firefighters love the media because you always make us look good. We normally do our best to give you what you need, but in this case, I just can't let there be a chance of this child's family learning about his death on TV. I wouldn't want something like that to happen to my family or to any of yours!"

I got a bunch of blank stares, so I wasn't sure what to think. Then, without warning, the physically largest videographer slowly lowered his camera and said, "I didn't even think of that. I'm glad you made that decision, because I wouldn't want that to happen to my family, either."

Without another word from the group, they quickly turned their cameras and tripods. I looked over my shoulder and saw the coroner's van backing down the driveway toward the street. As the van drove away, the cameras were rolling. The reporters were all happy—they got their shot.

My decision and how I handled the situation was observed by the entire firefighting team. My leadership experience allowed me to control my own emotions to deal with the news media. I also used that same emotion to inspire a desired response in the thinking of this group of media professionals. To be fair, it must be stated that these members of the news media were there to do a job that held certain expectations of them. Much like the firefighters were there to do a job that involved certain expectations.

I honestly didn't have anything against the media individuals involved. The fact is, the situation made for emotions that challenged my ability to speak in a manner that would produce the results that I was seeking. I had to remind myself that these reporters and camera operators did not see that young child lying in his bed. They had not experienced that deeply emotional sight and were not dealing with the same level of emotion that all the firefighters were dealing with. Realizing this made dealing with their somewhat callous demeanor easier to handle.

Team leaders must be in control of their emotions at all times, even if the team members are dealing with a very difficult and emotional situation. When necessary, leaders can deal with their personal feelings and emotions once the team has made it through the immediate situation. For leaders, emotional control cannot be overstated. How does this relate to you?

We all have moments, some more than others, where we get upset or frustrated with the situation we find ourselves in. The way we react to these situations is full of opportunities and dangers. What you say and how you say it will make the difference. Will you demonstrate influential leadership, or will you fail to lead? If you are a yeller, control your emotions. The relationship damage that can occur is too costly to continue to try to demand compliance by yelling louder. When this happens, no one is listening to a thing that is being said.

As a fire officer, I followed the "midnight rule." This meant that if something happened after midnight that was upsetting to me, I would wait until the next shift to discuss it with my team. What is your equivalent midnight rule? Is it Monday mornings, late afternoons, or when you haven't eaten? Think about it and identify when you are at your emotional worst. And then take action to protect your inspirational leadership style with a few personal rules for how and when to deal with emotional issues.

A word of advice: No one, in any work environment, should suppress his or her emotions indefinitely. Firefighters of all ranks as well as people in many other professions must deal with a multitude of painful and heartbreaking situations throughout their careers. They remain professional and strong until they can deal with their emotions in a way that works for them. This should include professional counseling whenever necessary. Most organizations have access to an employee assistance program that can help out in this area.

Regardless of the situation that you may find yourself dealing with, doing the right things for the right reasons may not always be seen as the best business decision. It will, however, always produce the results that you and your team can be proud of.

## CPR + R² = Successful Business Teams

Whether you are the leader or a member of a team, there are some success principles that must be part of your thinking to become high performance. The principles found in the success formula CPR + $R^2$ are important for teams, because they provide the strategic critical thinking and will-do focus for each individual and for the team as a whole. This is critical so that distractions, such as overbearing personalities, don't create barriers to collective success.

When any team makes CPR + $R^2$ part of their process, high-performance teamwork will be the result. With this formula, your team will embrace the Class 1 Culture by having a process that ensures success by creating the vision to solve problems, developing effective planning skills, having dedication to be the best at what they do, and fostering the ability to continuously improve as team members search for best practices.

With everyone on a team being motivated by the same cultural attitudes, as presented throughout this book, what might happen if the team leader is suddenly unable to participate with the team? For example, there are times in firefighting where the leader (the lieutenant, captain, or chief) is not able to continue his or her current duties. This might be due to an injury, or there are times when that person is summoned to meet face-to-face at a command post to discuss a change in firefighting strategy or tactics, not to mention many various other reasons for sudden absence from the team. In business, there are just as many reasons why a team leader might become missing in action, leaving the team to fend for themselves.

To ensure that a high-performance team will always be able to perform, the fire service culture requires team members to be trained and prepared to move up into the vacant leadership position. This is possible because there is always a plan to answer the what-ifs. There are no questions asked and no debate. When the leader is taken out of the situation, another member of the firefighting team steps in, as preplanned, so that the mission never fails. This is an example of high-performance teamwork demonstrating the will-do attitude.

---

### 🔥 Hot Tip

Leadership is all about helping others to succeed, and preparing for success simply means that you must continuously develop the members of your team.

---

How do I know that all of this works to create high-performance teams? I was the commander of the Air Operations Section for two years, including the evening when the disastrous fire occurred at the First Interstate Bank Building. I was not on duty that particular night, so I did not respond to this emergency. However, I did watch it on the late-night television news like all of the other interested viewers. As I sat and watched the news coverage, I really wanted to be there, right in the middle of it with my team. It was one of those uncomfortable moments where I could only observe.

As I followed the news coverage, I had absolute confidence in each individual on the responding teams because I was fully aware of the dedication, skill, and courage that each of them would bring to the challenges being encountered. I knew that the Air Operation teams would come together in the will do style, which is the norm for any organization with a culture that provides mission, vision, and values to guide and to inspire.

There are times when leading from the front is necessary. A leader can't lead with the you go . . . I go teamwork example if the team never sees how that person makes decisions or how he or she performs and responds in different scenarios. But leadership is all about helping others to succeed. Preparing for success means that, unless we work alone, we must continuously develop the members of our team to step in and move up when necessary. With the right principles in place, leaders can have faith in their teams to do the right things for the right reasons and at the right time, even when those leaders aren't physically present.

When we empower our teams with the expectation and authority to respond with a focused will-do attitude, there are times when we can and should lead from the rear. We can even lead from our living room sofa, watching the action on TV while appreciating the hard-earned success of others.

## Chapter Review: Empower Your People

The following is a review of how you can create high-performance teamwork.

The basic needs for creating a high-performance team are:

People + Desire + Trusted Leadership = Teamwork

In addition to these basics, to build the foundation for a high-performance team requires the following critical components:

- Mission to Motivation
- Vision to Reality
- Values for All
- Trusted Inspirational Leadership
- Doing the Right Things for the Right Reasons

- CPR + $R^2$ = Successful Business Teams
- Class 1 Culture

## Revise: This Is Your Call to Action

1. What will you do differently in your work and in your life?
2. What is the size and scope of how you propose to improve?

## Note

1. The LAFD utilized airborne engine companies throughout the 1980s. They were initially developed in preparation for emergency response planning for the 1984 Summer Olympics in Los Angeles. There were two engine companies with this designation, each with a team of four firefighting personnel specially trained and equipped for helicopter fire and rescue operations.

# 5

# 10 Success Orders for Business Firefighting

*Do the hard jobs first. The easy jobs will take care of themselves.*

—Dale Carnegie

It was a beautifully clear, hot and sunny autumn day; the on-duty firefighters had just sat down to eat lunch, and then the alarm sounded. "Reported brush fire," the dispatcher announced. The entire crew jumped to their feet and ran for their assigned apparatus. We were now part of the initial firefighting response to a reported brush fire near Malibu Canyon.

As our 3 fire apparatuses rolled out of the station, each of the 10 firefighters had a look of awe as they gazed at the size of the smoke cloud—what firefighters refer to as a "header" or "loom-up"—forming off in the distance. We were all focused on this header with a base that appeared to be a mile wide and growing rapidly, with the smoke climbing many thousands of feet into the air.

The Santa Ana winds had been blowing for days, and now these winds—also known as "devil winds"—were pushing a conflagration through the brush-covered coastal mountains and canyons toward the Pacific Ocean. With our stomachs reminding us that it was still lunchtime, the single thought that had everyone's focus was that it would be our duty to try to steer the rapidly advancing flames around the people and the buildings along its sure-to-be-destructive path.

When confronted with a wind-driven wildfire, everyone's expectations change. Firefighting grows increasingly unpredictable and dangerous as the wind speed increases and the humidity drops. It is for this reason that fire engine crews are formed into strike teams, with each strike team consisting of five engines, all under the command of one battalion chief.

We arrived at a staging area, where we joined up with additional firefighting resources. Within minutes, we were assigned to a battalion chief and were then part of a strike team. Soon, we were all on our way into the unknown.

A strike team is flexible enough to respond quickly to save lives and work together to protect multiple buildings, and it can also spread out to cover a considerable amount of terrain when necessary. Being under the command of a single battalion chief allows for strategic planning for the entire strike team to follow. The captains commanding each of the five engine company crews also maintain the ability to lead their individual firefighting teams with tactics and methods dictated by the current or expected fire behavior. Strategic and tactical considerations and actions by each crew could include a hit-and-run or a dig-in-and-stay-put response, all while under the command and control of the strike-team leader.

Our strike team was responding north on California State Route 1, also known as the Pacific Coast Highway, and the locals refer to it as PCH. As we caravanned toward the leeward side of the then-exploding conflagration, the massive smoke cloud began to turn the blue sky to gray. As we responded closer to where the fire was expected to cross PCH, the smoke from the raging fire totally blocked out the sun. The hot dry air had the unique smell of burning Laurel sumac and scrub oak, both types of native vegetation currently fueling the inferno.

Our strike team's assignment was to respond into Las Flores Canyon, one of many canyons in the Santa Monica Mountains, with a goal to protect structures. With the battalion chief's command vehicle in the lead, my engine company was the last in line of the five engines. This gave me a great vantage point to observe the entire strike team.

As we reached the intersection of PCH and Las Flores Canyon Road, I could see the other four engines and the battalion chief's command vehicle come face-to-face with red tongues of fire. The wind-driven flames were licking the pavement of the highway and impinging on the cluster of buildings situated on both sides of the intersection.

In the southbound lanes of PCH, there was bumper-to-bumper traffic at a dead standstill. As the flames approached, I saw drivers and passengers inside the vehicles with absolute terror on their faces, each of them realizing that there was nowhere to go to escape with his or her life.

If we couldn't get this traffic moving, our first priority would be to do our best to protect the people trapped inside these vehicles. Because of the critical nature of the situation and with no time to spare, our strike-team leader gave an order over the radio. "Everyone, take an exposed vehicle or building, and protect it the best you can." The order was clear, and it was understood that every firefighting team was empowered to fulfill the mission of the fire service the best they could, albeit on their own.

Obviously, this situation had become a firefighting crisis. Whatever decisions were ultimately made, success would depend upon the firefighting tactics employed and the ability of these firefighting leaders to make the quick decisions that always carry with them the potential to deliver life or death. Let's take a look at how the culture and leadership of the fire service makes it possible for firefighters to be prepared to handle such a challenging situation and how you can adapt the same principles to your organization to be prepared when a crisis strikes.

## Business Firefighting

When businesses find themselves in "firefighting mode," or crisis management, most would agree that it's a distraction from achieving planned priorities and accomplishing the daily routine. Would it surprise you to learn that the same is true for firefighters? We'll get to that later, but first let's review why organizations find themselves in firefighting mode in the first place.

The need to fight "business fires" can arise for a variety of reasons. In some cases, there are companies that have unknowingly developed a culture of crisis management, or business firefighting, which can give some people a feeling of greater value to the organization. The more fires they can successfully fight on their own, the more they get rewarded for saving the day.

In other cases, there are organizations of all types and sizes that don't have the necessary processes in place, that fail to learn from mistakes, and that tend to be reactive instead of proactive. There is a constant flow of business media reports about companies just like this. Without proper vision and planning, the same crises will occur—requiring the same firefighting reaction—over and over again.

There are also business cultures that expect the leaders or managers to always deal with the problems (fight the fires). This can create a workforce that doesn't take ownership for problems that occur. The mentality of "it's not my job" is a consequence of this type of dysfunctional culture. In most industries, this has been termed as the "silo effect."[1] The existence of this attitude can lead to the following: a lack of accountability, poor customer service, miscommunications, low motivation and morale, decreased productivity, dysfunctional teamwork, and an inferior work ethic. All these undesirable workforce traits will also add to the increased need to engage in business firefighting, also known as crisis management.

We have also found that business firefighting generally increases in organizations that have become extremely lean in human resources. This is a situation that has occurred extensively during economic downturns and, as we are currently experiencing, slow recoveries. Good workers who are effective and efficient people—business firefighters—are sometimes overwhelmed in their primary duties. This can be caused by their being forced to wear too many hats, resulting in disconnected accountabilities due to numerous responsibilities in a variety of areas. These people are constantly compelled to drop everything in order to address a business crisis and constantly trying to stomp out business spot fires. No amount of prevention will totally mitigate the risk of business fires until this lack of human resources is carefully and adequately addressed.

Perhaps it is safe to say that business firefighting is caused by as many different reasons as there are tasks, occupations, positions, or problems. A typical outcome when these business fires do break out is that they are at best disruptive and at worst destructive. So, prevention is always worth the effort.

When prevention fails, we must keep in mind that actual firefighting and business firefighting are team efforts, requiring everyone to be informed, to do his or her part, and to do it well.

## The Business of Firefighting

As firefighting in business goes, so goes firefighting for firefighters. The daily routine for today's professional firefighter is crammed with more tasks on their to-do-list than can actually be accomplished in a 24-hour workday. Firefighters are very successful at getting the right things done for the right reasons and at the right time. As we stress throughout this book, it is culture and leadership that have the power to improve, empower, and transform any organization to do the same.

When a firefighter reports to duty to start a shift, which can vary from 12 to 48 consecutive hours or more, he or she will prepare by first participating in what is known as "relief." This includes a brief meeting between the oncoming firefighter and the offgoing firefighter. Relief occurs with every assigned position and rank, with clear two-way communications being a must. The discussion includes the activities of the previous shift, including any incomplete work that has carried over to the succeeding shift and now requires attention by the oncoming team members.

The oncoming firefighter will safely stow the offgoing firefighter's personal protective gear and replace it with his or hers. The oncoming firefighter has now assumed the duties for that position on the fire engine, fire truck, or rescue ambulance. This is immediately followed by testing the operation of the self-contained breathing apparatus, and all other safety equipment and tools are examined during a complete inspection of the equipment inventory. Each individual coming on duty is expected to complete this inventory check to be personally certain that everything is in its proper place.

Most firefighters like to eat, so they take a quick nutrition detour to the kitchen, pour a cup of coffee, and then it's time for lineup. Lineup is a morning briefing that covers everything that the station commander wants to communicate to the crew. This briefing gets the shift started off right, with the entire on-duty crew hearing what the captain has planned for the day. This allows everyone to know the captain's vision for the shift. The information flow starts with a safety briefing, administrative news, plus the day's routine work schedule.

The daily routine tasks may include: specific training, apparatus and equipment maintenance and cleaning, fire station maintenance and cleaning, fire-prevention inspections, preresponse planning inspections, fire hydrant testing and maintenance, and more; the list can go on and on. The point is, if the alarm never sounds, the firefighting team members start their shift with more to do than they can accomplish. If the alarm does sound—and it usually does many times throughout the shift for all active fire and rescue companies—the assigned routine duties, including the tasks necessary to achieve longer-term goals, will not get done.

Yes, just as in business, firefighting is a distraction from the day's planned activities for firefighters. Fire commanders prepare for but do not plan their day around fires or other emergencies. This is because no one can predict exactly when the next alarm will sound. And no one can predict exactly when a business crisis will occur, either.

Preparation for any emergency is an important part of the entire firefighting team's day. However, the daily schedule does not have any actual time set aside for fires, rescues, or other emergencies. Life-threatening events will occur at any moment and without prior notice. Commanders are confident that when the alarm does sound, their firefighting teams are ready, willing, and able to drop everything and successfully respond to any emergency.

Once lineup is complete, all the firefighters will spend approximately an hour participating in an exercise program. Then they will dress for success in their work uniforms to begin their routine duties.

Just as in any business, firefighters have a proposed daily routine that has been designed to complete the necessary work assigned to that day of the week. Whenever fires do break out—whether metaphorical business fires or the actual red-hot flaming ones—the entire team must be constantly prepared to respond to fight them as well. Preparation and vigilance hastens a successful resolution, no matter what type of fire is being fought.

## What Is Your Definition of Success?

As previously described, firefighters battling a fire will define success as getting a knockdown. This is the moment when the fire has been extinguished—problem solved. There is still much work to do, but the urgency is over, and success has been achieved.

Achieving a knockdown is an important phase in the operation and must become known to the entire team engaged in fighting the fire. Firefighting is accomplished by the complementary efforts of many individuals and teams contributing to a vision for success through an organized and coordinated plan of attack. The incident commander is the chief officer and leader in command of the firefighting and rescue efforts. Because the IC controls every aspect of the incident, once a knockdown has been achieved, he or she will communicate this important information to all the teams involved.

When the IC announces over the radio for everyone on scene to hear, "We have a knock down," the dispatcher will also verbally announce the knockdown time for the official record of the incident. This communicates to every firefighter and command officer that success has been achieved. This is important because it tells everyone involved that the main problem has been solved and that there is no need to expose anyone to additional risk. There can now be a shift back to the routine, where there is a less critical focus.

It is equally important to follow this process in business. Think of your entire team going into crisis mode to knock down a problem, obstacle, or challenge (POC). Effectively, everyone is dropping everything in order to avert or solve the crisis. While the crisis is in play, the routine has been interrupted for everyone involved. Once the POC is solved (the business fire has been knocked down), the entire team needs to be alerted that the all clear has been called. This allows everyone to make the shift back to the routine. Depending upon your industry, any amount of downtime due to a crisis can be extremely costly to the company. Therefore, the sooner you achieve and communicate a knockdown, the better.

We have been very successful in our business careers through applying this approach to each crisis we faced. The former vice president of USA sales for Alberto Culver, Tom Nestor, says this about Bird's performance:

"A remarkable and innovative job of managing risk, with utmost integrity, communicating well within our company and our industry, and consistently delivered upon his commitments."

No matter the situation, Bird had learned these lessons during his firefighting career and continued to use these principles to achieve business success. Applying the same thinking to his business challenges allowed him to excel and to handle any crisis that came his way.

> ### 🔥 Hot Tip
>
> It is amazing just how easy it is to prevent most crisis situations by knowing what success looks like. All fires are destructive, so preventing "business fires" is always worth the effort.

After realizing his or her initial vision for fighting the fire, the IC will now develop a new vision for handling the remaining tasks still needing to be accomplished. Now, the entire firefighting team will shift from the critical mode, responding to save lives and protect property with a sense of urgency, to a more predictable routine response. The emergency has been abated, and we can now return to our routine tasks. For the firefighters and team leaders involved, this indicates the reorganization of on-scene resources to begin performing the overhaul and cleanup procedures.

The overhaul insures that the fire is out—it's cold—and that no rekindle can occur. It can be compared to a thorough follow-up with business clients to ensure the delivery of everything promised has occurred.

It is the leader's goal and responsibility to leave the affected premises in the best condition possible. In doing so, the mission to protect property continues to be served. This is also the time when all responders on scene start to prepare for the next alarm—the next customer. As diligently and efficiently as possible, the work begins with picking up hoselines, ladders, tools, equipment, and replenishing spent SCBA air cylinders. And then it's back to the routine work of the day until the next alarm sounds.

## Prevention Is Always Worth the Effort

The fire service is also dedicated to preventing fires from occurring in the first place. There is a great deal of effort put into fire-prevention inspections and community education. The fire-prevention inspections and fire-education programs are conducted by the same firefighters whose duty it is to respond to save lives and protect property. All of these additional duties, not related to fighting fires, are contributing to fulfill the same organizational mission.

The definition of success for fire-prevention efforts is to see a continuous drop in the numbers of fires, resulting in fewer fire injuries and fatalities. To save just one life because a smoke detector was installed or a battery was replaced equals success for prevention efforts. Prevention is always worth the effort, because it continues to fulfill the mission.

Preventing business fires is also always worth the effort. It is amazing just how easy it is to prevent most crisis situations by knowing what success looks like. For example, a few years ago, I saw a sign pinned to the bulletin board above the desk of an advertising salesman. The sign read, "I don't save lives . . . I just sell advertising." I read that sign and thought it was an odd thing to communicate, but I wasn't sure why I felt that way. Having worked in a profession that does save lives, I assumed that perhaps it was a compliment to all those who do save lives.

A few months later, I was sitting in the waiting area of a small local television station, moments away from walking into the studio to appear on a live talk show. I was distracted by an angry woman barging into the reception area, and in a not-so-friendly manner, she shouted at the receptionist, "We are having a make-or-break sale this weekend, and I just saw our TV and online ads, and you have the date wrong! You are advertising that our sale was last weekend!"

I suddenly found myself thinking back to that sign that said, "I don't save lives . . . I just sell advertising." I imagined another sign that might read, "I don't save lives . . . I just kill small businesses and destroy dreams."

I thought that in some way, advertising—or anything, for that matter—is more important than it may seem. If it's important enough to do, it's important enough to do it right. If it is your job, it is important enough to do it well. But whatever "it" is for you, it always matters to someone whether you have done it well.

This confrontation was a business fire that could have been prevented with a different definition of success for the sales staff involved. I wasn't positive, but I concluded that this media outlet probably didn't have a culture that expected their employees to live by the mission, vision, and values that a customer service–oriented company should have.

One of the basic realities propagated throughout today's business environment is the need to produce more, faster, and better products and services, but to produce them with fewer resources (people, things, money, and time) than they had before. When companies operate in this manner, something unexpected inevitably happens that will cause many people to go into firefighting mode. When this happens, does your team have a procedure to organize itself and surround the problem? Will your team automatically define what success looks like and then take action to quickly knock down the flames of crisis?

Organizations must focus on rapid and effective actions when the unexpected problems arise. Leaders must commit to a cultural change to produce an environment that values teamwork when the business firefighting alarm sounds.

## Effective versus Efficient

It is essential for leaders reading this book to consider something that sets firefighting apart from most other professions. For actual firefighting, there are so many variables encountered that each emergency incident is unique. Because of this, it is nearly impossible to accurately measure efficiencies. The same is possibly true for most organizations when they find themselves in crisis mode.

Over the past decades, there have been many studies conducted by different agencies to calculate what the most efficient staffing levels are for a firefighting team. Some studies have also tried to define what the most efficient strategies and tactics are to employ for certain firefighting situations.

There are many opinions that are based on testing these and other subjects related to firefighting efficiencies. However, these tests fail to reflect what actually occurs in real-life firefighting and rescue situations. In the real world of firefighting, it is effectiveness that really matters.

In similar ways, there are also many variables involved with crisis management. In business, what is *effective* during business firefighting is more important and possible to measure than what is *efficient*. For example, efficiency is measureable in routine business production when every detail can be planned and scrutinized for the most efficient use of resources. Now, just imagine a crisis where the production process is on fire. We believe that the only meaningful measurement in this scenario is whether you are effective in extinguishing the fire and saving the production process. A crisis is a crisis, and being effective at handling it is the measurement that counts.

## Standard Operating Procedures

We have previously covered the importance of standard operating procedures, but the importance of SOPs for dealing with a crisis deserves additional discussion here. Firefighters are usually the first responders arriving not only to fires but also to nearly every type of emergency imaginable. Every emergency has its own challenges, and the fire service relies on standard operating procedures to bring these situations to a successful close. Having SOPs to follow are like knowing the game plan before the game even starts or before your opponents even arrive.

It is beneficial to develop SOPs in business that can serve as a game plan for your business firefighting mode. As in most emergency scenarios, some people will resort to what they've been taught to do in order to handle the situation. This is sometimes referred to as "muscle memory," which is achieved by developing good habits like using the stairs instead of the elevator when the fire alarm sounds without thinking about it consciously. On the other hand, there are some people who will resort to panic. These individuals are usually the ones who haven't received adequate training.

SOPs provide specific guidelines for your entire team to follow in a variety of different situations. Training on SOPs can assure that good things will have a greater chance of occurring when bad things happen. No matter what assignment is given, by following well-established SOPs, everyone will be working collectively in a coordinated effort to handle the emergency or crisis.

SOPs may be a modification for how business firefighting is currently accomplished in your organization. However, successful crisis management in any organization requires a change in thinking from the routine.

## Devil Winds and Crisis Management

Similar to when a crisis requires a shift in thinking for various business situations, when autumn brings on a shift in prevailing wind patterns, it will change how firefighters think and act as they perform their duties. In Southern California, these wind patterns are called Santa Ana winds, and they drive the fierce firestorms that race across wildlands and populated communities all too often.

These hot, dry winds have a huge impact on expected fire behavior. When these weather patterns occur, firefighters must adjust how they do business. Consequently, firefighting strategies and tactics must be modified to manage the extreme burning conditions that accompany wind-driven fires. This is a crisis situation for firefighters and a perfect place to return to our opening firestorm at PCH and Las Flores Canyon Road.

By the time my engine advanced to the intersection, the other four engine crews were pulling hoselines and hooking up to nearby fire hydrants for water supplies. Each building was being defended by at least one firefighter. The southbound traffic had now begun to move quickly away from danger. Law enforcement officers had shut down the northbound lanes, allowing these understandably frightened people to drive their vehicles in the now empty lanes to escape the flames.

My engine came to a stop at the intersection of PCH and Las Flores Canyon. Taking a moment to consider the entire situation, I looked up the canyon road in the direction the fire was coming from. I could see multiple homes and a two-story apartment building that would surely be lost to the flames without protective actions. I knew that the fire behavior was extreme and unpredictable. So before committing my crew to action, I gave a quick thought to the 10 Standard Firefighting Orders[2] and how they could be applied to this crisis situation that I was planning to engage.

> **🔥 Hot Tip**
>
> Successful crisis management in any organization requires a change in thinking from the routine.

These 10 orders have been in place since 1957 and were developed to keep firefighters as safe as possible when involved in very dangerous work. They are the product of many years of wildland firefighting experience, and they are the result of countless review-and-revise process discussions and continuous incremental improvements to firefighting operations during crisis situations.

As we have stated in this book many times, the fire service reviews every incident. Whenever improvement to operations or safety is possible, fire service leaders revise operational standards as the lessons learned so indicate. These revisions become the newly discovered best practices for all to follow. The process has been a success for wildland firefighting and for many other operational procedures throughout the fire service. This list is a great example of how $R^2$ is utilized to improve fire service safety and operational outcomes. Each order represents the lessons learned by firefighters who had suffered from thousands of burn injuries and, for some, lost their lives trying to save the lives and property of others. For the affected firefighters and their families, these were hard lessons to learn and to endure.

Due to the identification of the causes of earlier firefighting tragedies, with a process like $R^2$, firefighters now have this list to follow in order to improve on their safety and their success and to help protect their lives. The

10-order list is a tool to help prevent, or at least greatly reduce, future line-of-duty deaths and injuries.

Faced with the challenges presented by this Las Flores Canyon inferno, I would rely on this list for assisting my ability to manage, lead, and safeguard my crew. The winds were raging down the canyon at over 50 miles per hour, rapidly driving the flames toward our location and delivering a steady barrage of firebrands ripping through the air. As I began to take command of how best to proceed, it was the safety of my crew that was my first concern. My next concern was how best to serve our mission.

I knew if we could establish a reliable water supply, we could get aggressive and possibly save the apartment building and maybe even some of the neighboring homes. Adjacent to where we had stopped was a fire hydrant. One of my crew members made a quick check, and the hydrant had a strong water supply; we were in business!

I quickly informed the crew of my plan. Utilizing two-way communication, I was confident that they all understood our task and the challenges at hand. I transmitted a radio message to the strike-team leader with the same information. Without hesitation, the chief gave me the confident-sounding reply, "Roger. Go ahead!"

We attached our fire engine's water supply hoseline to the hydrant. With fire all around us, we drove up the narrow canyon road, laying a three-and-a-half-inch diameter hoseline that would deliver us the water we needed to protect the threatened buildings and ourselves. Stopping in front of the apartment building, I climbed down off of the engine and saw that we had used our entire complement of 600 feet of supply hose. It was apparent to the entire team that we needed to hurry, as upon our arrival, we could see that the fire had already ignited the roof eaves at the rear of the apartment building.

One of the firefighters ran through the apartment lobby, dragging a hoseline all the way into the rear courtyard. Using a sweeping motion with the water stream from the nozzle, he quickly beat back the flames that were consuming the eaves. His actions narrowly prevented the fire from breaking out the windows on the second floor. If the fire had broken out these windows, the flaming embers would have ignited the interior of the building, resulting in almost certain total destruction.

Simultaneously, another firefighter pulled a hoseline to a house on the west side of the apartment building. With flames igniting the nearby vegetation, this man put himself in position to protect the house and the west side of the apartment complex. During these firefighting maneuvers, our engineer was busy hooking up his water supply, coupling and uncoupling hoses, hooking lines to the fire engine's pump, and providing the water pressure necessary to feed the various firefighting hoselines that were now in operation.

With the entire crew already engaged in firefighting, another firefighter extended a hoseline to the east side of the apartment to protect another neighboring house. I also pulled an additional hoseline across the street to protect two more houses. This hoseline was in place, but because I would be continuously patrolling the area in order to maintain situational awareness, I would not be able to remain in that position. Should any embers ignite these structures, this hoseline would be already available and in place for one of my team members to quickly knock down the flames. And this was almost certain to occur due to the wind-driven flames and embers now bearing down upon us.

The conditions were treacherous as the main fire—with up to 100-foot flame lengths—was being forced through this canyon by the hot, erratic winds. It was apparent why these winds had earned the name "devil winds."

It was also apparent that I needed to employ more of the 10 standard firefighting orders. I transmitted another radio message to my strike team leader with my PPN. This communicated to him that we were in our assigned location (*position*) with a good water supply and successfully protecting the apartment building (*progress*), and that if I could get additional engine companies to our location (*needs*), we could save even more homes.

Just in case the flames became too hot for us to endure, I determined that the safety zone for my crew was in the lobby of the apartment building. I told each firefighter the route they should take if they needed to escape to the safety zone. I was the team's lookout, and each firefighter knew that I was patrolling the area of operation and that we would communicate with each other about any additional hazardous situations that may arise. Firefighters refer to these four important information details as LCES, an acronym for lookouts, communications, escape routes, and safety zones. These principles are all part of the 10 standard firefighting orders and are all considered a critical necessity to keep everyone as safe as possible.

In response to my PPN request for assistance, our strike-team leader radioed me and reported that he was sending us one additional engine company to assist with structure protection. This was a satisfying and prompt result from the communication practice of utilizing PPN. Eventually, the arriving engine company was visible, moving slowly along the dark, smoke-obscured canyon road. I assigned this engine team to the four additional houses east of my crew's location. I was expected to maintain control of the entire firefighting effort in my operational area, and the 10 firefighting orders allowed me to meet those expectations.

This fire siege lasted nearly five hours before it was safe enough to announce a knockdown in this operational sector. The flames had finally consumed most of the available fuel—the brush and trees that had once beautified the hillsides—but not the structures that had been successfully protected. The official Los Angeles County Fire Department's record of this fire stated, in part:

> It became apparent that . . . the Las Flores Canyons would be struck hard. The winds were blowing at 50 miles per hour and the fire had become a four mile wide monster that was devouring canyons in its path like a machine. . . . Despite the apocalyptic eeriness which lay before them, engine companies ascended into these canyons courageously, as safety would allow. Their experiences will no doubt impact them profoundly for the remainder of their lives.

Throughout this challenging situation, every crew member stayed alert, kept calm, maintained clear thinking, and acted decisively. The end result for this small portion of a much larger conflagration was that the dwellings for over 25 families escaped destruction, and no civilians or firefighters were injured. Our strike team eventually continued on to several other locations, protecting more homes and businesses threatened by this same wildland fire.

## "You Go . . . I Go!"

Does this story sound anything like a "firefighting" story in your world? Things don't go exactly as planned, the unexpected happens, and suddenly you are engaged in crisis management or business firefighting with the need to stomp out brush fires.

As previously noted, when fires do break out, it is best for the entire team to go to work on the problem. Can you imagine just me, trying to be the heroic leader and fight that fire by myself, leaving the rest of my crew at the fire station to carry on with the daily routine station duties? Well, first of all, none of the firefighters would have wanted to stay behind to do the routine when the critical needed to be addressed. Firefighters are committed to the team concept and believe in the buddy system. To put it another way, many firefighters have a favorite saying, "You go . . . I go!" And they mean it.

Second, I would not have been successful going it solo. In fact, because I wouldn't have been able to safely respond into the canyon by myself, all of the property that was saved would have surely been lost to the fire. Working as a team produced the synergy needed to get a knockdown on the crisis as quickly as possible. Teamwork allowed everyone to get back to the routine quicker by working together to deal with the crisis at hand.

---

### 🔥 Hot Tip

Like an out-of-control fire, the longer a business problem is allowed to continue, the bigger and more destructive it will become. Diligence to duty dictates actions must be taken, as a team, to protect your business from harm.

---

## 10 Success Orders for Business Firefighting

Like in a fire station, in business, critical situations or emergencies happen, and people must respond. In your profession, this might earn someone the title of "business firefighter." The following list of 10 Success Orders for Business Firefighting has been adapted from the actual list of 10 standard firefighting orders, previously cited.

Hopefully the fires that break out in your organization aren't the hot and smoky ones. Instead, they are probably the urgent situations that occur, and if not handled immediately, serious business damage can be the result. This following list of things to do during a crisis will help to quickly knock down the flames of trouble. More importantly, they can also help to prevent these business fires from breaking out in the first place.

Remember that prevention is always worth the effort. Successful business firefighting starts with an SOP to follow specific orders, or a checklist, to prevent the very issues that cause business fires. When the fires of crisis do ignite, and they will, the life-saving orders that firefighters use to protect themselves have been customized and adapted for business. When needed, use them to protect yourself, your team, and your entire organization.

When anyone is stressed in a crisis situation, he or she needs more information; this person needs and wants details. Having a checklist that works in your organization—preplanned—keeps people from guessing what to do at times of tremendous stress and difficulties. These firefighting principles are known as the 10 Success Orders for Business Firefighting. They are relevant for your crisis management to resolve the crisis. They are also useful for your prevention efforts to avert a crisis.

As you read through the list, try to take ownership of these orders by identifying how your organization could apply them during a crisis situation. Also, consider their application on an ongoing basis to prevent problems before they happen in your specific business task, occupation, position, or environment.

F—Fight business fires aggressively, but provide for safety first.
- Aggressively take actions to address the problem and to ensure and maintain the professional and personal safety of all engaged team members as well as the organization.

I—Initiate all actions based on current and expected business fire behavior.
- Direct necessary resources to resolve the crisis as you understand it to be.
  - o Utilize CPR for Business to identify, prioritize, and manage POCs.

R—Recognize current business "weather conditions" and obtain forecasts.
- Are there business climate conditions that are occurring—or may occur—that are the same or similar to those that have caused problems in the past?
  - o What is on the horizon for your organization or in your industry? Consider: history, competition, market status, economy, and resources.

E—Ensure business instructions are given and understood.
- Establish two-way communications and maintain clear, concise, and accurate messaging procedures (PPN).
  - o Document communication history of instructions, compliance, questions, and answers.

O—Obtain current information on business fire status.
- What further needs to be addressed, if anything?
  - o Verify most current data pertaining to industry, category, brands, successes, failures, forecasts, and projections.

R—Remain in communication with engaged business team members, your supervisor, and cross-functional business units.
- Communicate clearly in all directions to ensure everyone involved is constantly and clearly informed to prevent problems.
  - o If problems occur, ensure all appropriate associates become engaged with resolving as soon as problems are identified.
  - o When the problem has been knocked down, communicate instructions for all engaged employees to return to their routine work.

D—Determine business safety zones and escape routes.
- Identify worst case scenario, and then define what safety is for the organization and the procedures to achieve it: exit strategies, financial, operational, political, and so forth.

E—Establish business lookouts in potentially hazardous situations.
- Identify someone as the lookout, who is responsible for monitoring agreed-upon metrics and potential hazards or threats, and announcing: progress or results, POCs, and early warning signs or symptoms.

R—Retain control of business at all times.
  • Maintain control of all aspects for continuing business, while controlling actions to successfully manage the crisis.
S—Stay alert, keep calm, think clearly, and act decisively.
  • If your entire team consistently does this, business fires can be prevented. When crisis strikes, this order will bring about the quickest possible knockdown every time.

You have probably discovered that these 10 Success Orders for Business Firefighting spell out "fire orders." This is just another way we try to help make these useful principles easier for everyone to remember when crisis strikes. Keep a copy of this book handy to have the principles at the ready when needed. Make a tab or dog-ear the page so that you and your team can quickly refer to these 10 success orders.

Even better, use these success orders as a template to customize your own crisis procedures. It doesn't matter what you call it or how it ends up looking. What matters is that it works by making a positive difference in how your organization responds to a crisis.

Here is an example of how I adapted these success orders to serve my work situation and to make a difference while working in a business leadership position.

The worst crisis for any company or organization is when an employee has been physically injured or killed. While working in business as a regional director for an air medical transport company, one afternoon I received a call from our communications center that no one wants to get. One of my helicopter crews put out a radio call for a possible in-flight emergency and reported that they were making a precautionary landing. Knowing that this could be anything from a false alarm to a catastrophic and deadly event, I quickly and confidently went into crisis mode.

Utilizing the 10 Success Orders for Business Firefighting as a guide, I was able to communicate with the right people and receive the information I needed to plan my next steps.

With an injured patient onboard, the flight crew had heard an unfamiliar sound upon liftoff from the scene of a traffic accident. They decided to set down in a safe location to further investigate the unidentifiable noise. Gratefully, this event was precautionary and was an excellent decision made by the crew.

After a brief inspection, the unfamiliar noise turned out to be a seatbelt hanging outside of the aircraft door, subsequently slapping the side of the fuselage in flight. The flight crew's actions were consistent with a company SOP that is also an aviation best practice for dealing with mechanical concerns while airborne: Investigate on the ground.

The 10 Success Orders allowed me to make the proper notifications, preparing for the worst case scenario, while also hoping for the best. Having this list to guide my thoughts and actions during this potential crisis allowed me to stay alert, keep calm, think clearly, and act decisively—all good and useful traits in times of crisis.

In the fire service as in business, firefighting can be a hazardous endeavor. Yet, to allow a fire to burn freely or a business problem to go unsolved is unacceptable. The longer a fire burns or a problem festers, the bigger and more destructive it will become. Diligence to duty dictates actions must be taken as a team to protect your business from harm. Having the right checklist available inspires people to take appropriate actions to address the problems, obstacles, and challenges that create crises. When business fires do break out and a crisis suddenly needs to be managed, use these 10 Success Orders for Business Firefighting to get a quick knockdown and then get back to work.

## Chapter Review: Empower Your People

Regardless of whether we are talking about actual fires or business fires, they all must be dealt with as quickly as possible and, wherever possible, they must be prevented in the first place.

The key points of this chapter are:

- (Business) fires are destructive.
- Prevention is always worth the effort.
- (Business) firefighting is a team endeavor.

Here is a review of important considerations for your crisis management:

1. Business Firefighting: In every business, there are problems that occur. Many times, these problems result from a lack of vigilance or situational awareness, poor communications, or an inability to make decisions.
2. What Is Your Definition of Success?: Defining success for the crisis at hand ensures that your team will always be able to prioritize the problems and limit the damage.
3. Effective versus Efficient: When dealing with a crisis-management situation, it is imperative to realize that being effective is more significant than being efficient. Because these crisis situations are hopefully not the norm, you should be more interested in how effectively the problem is being corrected and less concerned about the efficiency of the correction process. A crisis is a crisis, and effectively resolving the issue is the important measurement that matters.

4. Standard Operating Procedures: People will usually unconsciously resort to how they have been trained when managing a crisis or when dealing with emergency situations. SOPs provide specific guidelines for your entire team to perform during a crisis.

5. "You go . . . I go!": Firefighters are dedicated to the buddy system, and they work together to fight fires or rescue victims. You and your teams also need to work together to fight business fires. The team concept of "You go . . . I go!" is a collective attitude that believes we do better by working together.

6. 10 Success Orders for Business Firefighting: Keep this list of success orders at the ready. Remember that prevention is always worth the effort. Successful business firefighting starts with an SOP to follow these orders to help prevent the very issues that are causing the business fires before they occur. When a crisis does break out, the 10 success orders will be your guide as you handle the problems, helping you to get back to your routine work as soon as possible.

As you read and reread these orders, try to see how the following organizational challenges can be positively influenced:

- Leadership
- Teamwork
- Situational Awareness
- Communications
- Decision Making
- Continuous Improvements

When business fires do break out, give your teams a process to drop everything and come together to fight and successfully manage the flames of crisis. The destructive nature of any fire is just too great to leave this to chance.

### Revise: This Is Your Call to Action

1. What will you do differently in your work and in your life?
2. What is the size and scope of how you propose to improve?

### Notes

1. Dr. Sharon M. Biggs. *The Silo Effect: Invisible Barriers That Can Destroy Organizational Teams.* Sharon Biggs Publication, 2014.
2. The original ten Standard Firefighting Orders were developed in 1957 by a task force commissioned by the USDA—Forest Service Chief Richard E. McArdle. http://www.fs.fed.us/fire/safety/10-18/10-18.html

# 6

# Goal Assurance System

*Fanaticism consists of redoubling your efforts when you have forgotten your aim.*

—George Santayana

It was about midnight as we drove through the alley toward the three-story apartment building. I could see flames rolling out from the fire escape doors on the second and third floors. There was thick black smoke puffing out of every opening: windows, roof vents, and even the cracks in the mortar between the bricks of the exterior walls. It was obvious to all of the first responders that this apartment building full of occupants was heavily involved with deadly flames and smoke spreading rapidly throughout its interior.

My engine company captain initially directed me to extend a hoseline into a position that would allow my team to push back the flames coming from the second-floor fire escape balcony. His plan was developed to fulfill his directive from the incident commander: "Attack the fire on the second floor."

Our captain explained that once the flames were no longer engulfing the fire escape balcony, we would be able to raise a ladder up and into position. Climbing the ladder with a hoseline and nozzle, we could then advance into the building and down the hallway, knocking down the flames as we moved farther into the burning structure.

Our captain had communicated his vision to our team. He then identified the firefighting evolutions—the plan—we would use to transform his vision into reality. We prepared to accept our piece of the overall firefighting and rescue effort. Everyone on our entire firefighting team understood his individual responsibilities, including our goal as a group for what we were about to accomplish.

I looked toward the fire escape to determine where I would have the best chance at effectively doing as I had been instructed. I saw that the flames filled the doorway that led to the second-floor hallway. The iron railing on the balcony was glowing red as though it was being heated by a welder's torch.

While I was pulling the hoseline into position, I heard a voice calling for help. I looked up and saw a man covered with soot, aggressively ripping the bug screen from the window opening where he was struggling to breathe, trying to escape from the smoke that filled his third-floor apartment.

For a moment, I thought about dropping the hose to alter my course of action. I struggled with the thought, *Should I get a ladder to save this guy?* My assignment, which became my goal, was to knock down the fire on the second floor. Other firefighters were involved with activities to get a knock-down on the third floor. If I failed to accomplish my given task, my goal— our team responsibility—would not be achieved.

Those firefighters going to the third floor to save lives were counting on our engine company's successful extinguishment of the second-floor fire. If we were delayed and failed to achieve our goal, the entire third floor could collapse into the second floor, possibly taking many lives, including the lives of those firefighters.

I chose to continue with the hoseline to my preplanned position. I opened the nozzle while leaning forward with all my might to fight against the nozzle reaction, the backward force caused by the powerful stream of water ejecting from the nozzle toward the target. I successfully pushed back the flames.

My captain, along with the other firefighter on our team, raised a ladder up and into position on the fire escape balcony. I ran up the ladder with an interior attack hoseline and nozzle slung over my right shoulder. Once on the fire escape balcony, I continued to pull additional hose up to my location. This would give us adequate line to make our way deep into the second-floor hallway.

Standing on the fire escape balcony and prior to entering the second-floor hallway, I looked over to the man still in his third-floor window. He was trying to breathe fresh air by extending his head and upper torso as far out of the window as he could and doing his best to cling to life, yet he was so close to falling. I saw a firefighter from another fire company carrying a ladder toward the side of the building where the man was located. He pushed the ladder up into position to rescue the man, who now appeared to be very close to jumping.

The firefighter carrying the heavy ladder was part of a truck company. In addition to a large assortment of rescue and ventilation tools, a truck company also carries a large complement of ladders. At this emergency, the truck company to which this firefighter was assigned had been given the task of window rescues.

This man was just one of the many occupants who were saved that night from their apartment windows. The man in the third-floor window was saved, but not by me. I had been given a different assignment as part of this firefighting operational plan, which included specific tasks and required over a hundred firefighters to accomplish.

What might have happened if I had changed course in the middle of my assigned task—not quite done with one job, and dropping everything to attempt another? As difficult of a decision that the man in the window created for me, I was able to do the right thing by using the very same thought process that every firefighter working at this emergency would use to develop his or her course of action—the tactics and methods required—depending upon that person's assignments. This was also the same thought process that my captain employed to develop the tactics necessary to accomplish our team's assignment.

I used the same thought process that makes it possible to face the chaos of disasters like this fire. The thought process enables all of us to think clearly on our feet and to get the right things done for the right reasons—especially when we are dealing with competing priorities!

Even with the power of thought for critical thinking and analysis that comes from the success formula CPR plus $R^2$ or the benefits that the 10 Success Orders for Business Firefighting provide during times of crisis, there are times when we need the ability to maintain our focus on our goals while on the run. This process begins with understanding what the goal is, a step that is primary to achieving it.

Just as important as defining your goal is owning a thought process that provides conscious visualization of whatever it is that you are trying to do. When you can see your goal with your mind's-eye, your mind can dismiss all of the noise, distractions, and competing priorities, thereby allowing you to focus on goal achievement.

## What Is the Goal?

In 1993, Southern California suffered through a string of wildland fires that had the fire services stretched to the breaking point. The damage was great, but the firefighters came through, as they have always done, to save many lives and a great deal of property.

In appreciation for the fire service efforts, former president Ronald Reagan invited all firefighters and their families to attend a celebrated event at his presidential library in Simi Valley, California. I attended this event with hundreds of firefighters and their families, bringing along my youngest son, who was 10 years old at the time. I thought it would be a good opportunity for him to see one of our country's former presidents in person.

During the event, after President Reagan had addressed the group, he was given a fire chief's helmet from one of the many fire departments in attendance. Reagan placed the helmet on his head and thanked the crowd of firefighters and their family members. My best recollection is that he said, "I have accomplished a great many goals in my life, but one of the first things that I ever wanted to become was a firefighter . . . a goal," he concluded, "I never was able to achieve." He added, "At least I now have the helmet!"

He took the helmet off of his head, pointed it toward the crowd, and said, "My hat is off to all of you for your dedicated and courageous service for the people of California!" President Reagan's words made my son think that I was pretty special. I could only think that he was playing up his desire to be a firefighter to this particular audience. However, I do believe he was sincere in his respect for the job that firefighters do. I also believe that the many things that he did achieve during his well-documented and accomplished life started by his answering the question, what is the goal?

### 🔥 Hot Tip

By getting into the habit of identifying the goal in everything you do, you will discover that you are not only achieving your goals but also accomplishing them much sooner.

## Finding Your Focus

There is a great deal of noise and distraction at every emergency scene to which firefighters respond. They hear sounds of sirens, the roar of heavy apparatus engines, horns, radio messages, power saws, firefighters hollering over the noise, people screaming for help, and the deafening roar of a large building being consumed by fire. It is loud and distracting to be sure.

But firefighting is only one of the many professions that require the ability to be able to stay focused on the goal, even at times of terrific distractions, stress, and competing interests.

Have you ever taken on a simple task without being sure of the goal for your actions? Whether you are writing an e-mail or making a phone call to a business associate or client, there needs to be some thought process to ask the question, "Why am I doing this?"

Anyone can be much more productive when he or she takes a moment to think, "What is the goal?" By getting into the habit of identifying the goal in everything you do, you will discover that you are not only achieving your goals, you are accomplishing them sooner.

One reason why some people don't achieve goals is that they don't set goals. I can assure you that without knowing my goal was to knock down the fire on the second floor of the apartment building, I would have lost my focus. I would have dropped the hoseline and run off to find a ladder and done my best to rescue the man in the third-floor window. I would have done this, ignorant to the fact that others had been assigned this particular piece of the incident action plan. Trying to save the man clinging to life would have seemingly been the noble thing to do, but would it have been the right thing to do under the circumstances?

As previously pointed out, had I not maintained my focus to assure that my goal would be achieved, my actions could have been disastrous and cost many others their lives. These lives could have included an unknown number of occupants needing to be rescued as well as other firefighters working to save lives by knocking down the fire on the third floor.

The incident commander would have never committed firefighters to the third floor without first assigning the task of fire attack on the second floor. The reasoning is that as the fire burns, it is destroying the structural components that support the building itself. Prior to committing firefighters to a floor above the fire, the IC will want to be assured that other firefighters are already in the process of attacking the fire on the floors below and, hopefully, getting a quick knockdown.

Goals are obviously important for the life-or-death decisions firefighters must make. Goals are also critical for assuring that the moment-to-moment tasks assigned to anyone, in any line of work, are being accomplished. We can exchange the word "goal" with words like "objectives, needs, wants, desires, hopes, and dreams." These are all mindful thoughts of things that we want to see happen. Arguably, these are all goals.

The following will explain how to use a simple but effective thought process for goal assurance. It is a tactical system designed to assure we can successfully achieve our goals, no matter what we want to call them. The Goal Assurance System, or GAS, admittedly is a funny name for a tool that can deliver great success. So enjoy the humor, and then realize that being stranded without goals on the road of life isn't funny at all. But thankfully, being stranded anywhere and not knowing which way to turn can be prevented. You just need to get in the habit of finding your focus by always asking, "What is the goal?"

This system will assure that you succeed at achieving goals. It's much like getting into your car, and just by force of habit, you check the gas gauge to be certain that you can make it to your destination—your goal.

## A Mind's Eye View

Our destination is to take a look at a system that is so simple, it will change the way you think. GAS is a continuous mental process that allows you to evaluate what is known, while also seeking what is unknown. Once it becomes second nature for you, the success brought about by goal setting and achievement will be yours.

### Step One: What Is the Goal?

By knowing precisely what you want to achieve, you will know where you need to focus your efforts. The more specific you can be about your goal, the greater your level of success will be. This is because once we have visualized something that doesn't yet exist, it causes our subconscious mind to help us make the decisions necessary to make that visualized goal a reality.

Take a look at the triangle below. Close your eyes and think about the triangle with the word "goal" inside of it. The idea here is to develop an image in your mind's eye so it will be at your service when you need it. We want you to be able to have this process in the forefront of your mind so that you can use it on the go.

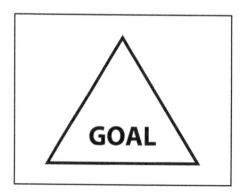

We emphasize the following:

1. Goals must clarify a specific action or outcome.
2. Goals must be measureable by being able to quantify the benefits of achieving them.
3. Goals should be achievable with the resources available (or at least you should know that the necessary resources are in reserve and can be acquired).
4. Goals must also be realistic for achieving based on your particular situation.
5. Goals must also include the time period in which you want to achieve them. With a date or time period specified for completion, planning can be established in order for evaluating the progress toward goal achievement, something that can be measured and quantified. A completion date or time also provides a structured continuum for planning the prioritized tasks that must be completed to achieve the goal. Without a time frame, it is all too easy to forget that you ever set the goal, thereby making it impossible to achieve.

## Step Two: Complete Your SIZE-UP

A SIZE-UP is the act of identifying what problems, obstacles, and challenges are in the way of assuring that your goal is achieved. When a firefighter, apparatus driver, captain, or battalion chief receives alarm information, each one begins a personal SIZE-UP. In the same way, depending on your place in the company or organization or your place in life, your SIZE-UP reflects your perspective of what you will need to do to achieve your stated goal.

Now, before we continue, stop here to look at the triangle below with the word "SIZE-UP." Follow the same process from step one to develop your mind's eye to visualize the triangle with SIZE-UP along the left slope.

When the fire chief arrived on the scene of the apartment fire, his organization's culture provided a mission to guide thought and action—how to set

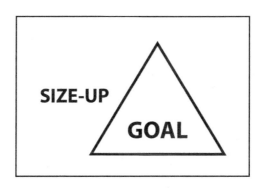

priorities—to save lives and protect property. Training and experience had provided the chief with a mental checklist for critical thinking, just like CPR plus $R^2$. This allowed for the development of an overall vision for the incident, effective planning to identify the strategies to be employed, and the assigning of the many tasks that would be carried out by the responding firefighting teams.

The captains in command of the fire companies responding to this incident employed a thought process that allowed them to focus on the goal for their specific firefighting team. The captains' goals for their teams would be defined depending upon the specific assignment each captain received from the incident commander.

The SIZE-UP Planning Process is explained in detail in chapter 2, but we also provide a brief explanation here. To facilitate using it on the go, we have created the following acronym: SIZE-UP.

S—See, Situation, Size and Scope
- See it either personally or with trusted eyes of another.
- Maintain situational awareness at all times.
- Evaluate the size and scope of problems, obstacles, or challenges (POCs) that need to be dealt with to achieve your goal.

I—Information
- Acquire accurate and current information, updating frequently.
- Never totally trust the first things you hear or assume that you have all of the information available. The more information you can find to identify POCs, the better your plan will be.

Z—Zero In
- Zero in on the causes of the POCs.
- Determine initial priority of tasks.
- Provide the solutions and actions necessary for goal achievement.

E—Environment and Exposures
- This is the 360-degree view of goal achievement.
- Every goal has six sides, like a box: There is a top, a bottom, and four sides. Everything inside the box is the environment where your plan for goal achievement must succeed.
- Everything outside of the box is the exposures, representing who or what may be impacted by your actions.

U—Uncover the Unknowns
- Surprises are usually disruptive, so look deeper to try to uncover the unknowns that could prevent your goal achievement.
- Ask questions about things that you think you know the answers to. And then listen carefully; the answers may uncover issues you had not even considered.

**P**—Planning
- The final step is to create a plan of action to achieve your goal.
- A successful plan identifies POCs.
- A successful plan also defines and prioritizes actions to mitigate POCs to achieve your goal.

The Size-Up Planning Process is flexible, practical, and useful enough to be implemented on the run to quickly assess the available information and then to rapidly create a plan of action. The same system is also designed to be utilized when you have a great deal of time, when there is no life-or-death urgency. Either way, using this process allows you to follow a plan that has identified actual problems, obstacles, and challenges that are standing between you and your goal. This way, your plan addresses specifically what needs to be done to solve, overcome, and conquer these issues to realize goal achievement.

## Step Three: Respond

Now that you have completed a size-up and have developed a plan that will lead you to achieve your goal, you must respond to that plan. For the fire service, the need to respond is always the action step for getting things done. The way that we respond also says a great deal about our culture: valuing teamwork; staying true to our mission, vision, and values; and getting the right things done for the right reasons by following the plan.

The same is true for business. As you respond to your plan to achieve your goals, remember to adhere to your organization's cultural norms. We assume that all organizations have the best intentions, but if cultural norms are not ethical, any goal achievement is diminished.

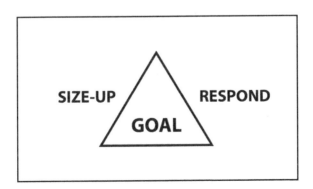

Okay, imagine that you are lifting that ladder and advancing that hose-line; it is as if you are firefighting now. Repeat the memory technique from the previous steps, and burn the above image into your memory.

### Step Four: $R^2$—Review and Revise

Once you have initiated your response, you must then move to the process previously covered in detail and referred to as $R^2$. During the review step of the $R^2$ Process, you evaluate the goal to decide if it has been achieved. If the answer is yes, you have accomplished your goal. Congratulations!

If you discover that the goal hasn't been achieved or if preliminary actions have failed, you complete the review to discover what worked and why and what didn't work and why. Then complete the revise step, which is your call to action to discover what you will do differently and the size and scope of how you propose to improve.

Armed with this updated information, move again to the beginning of the SIZE-UP Planning Process. This allows you to update your plan of action and establish revised actions based on the current situation.

Respond to the revised plan again, complete the $R^2$ process, and repeat it until you have achieved the goal.

During this process, you may even decide to alter the goal. This, of course, involves maintaining two-way communications with all associates that are engaged with achieving the same goal. Any updates or suggested changes need to be shared with your team immediately. This is a key to having team goal assurance, since most problems that result in any organization seem to come down to ineffective communications.

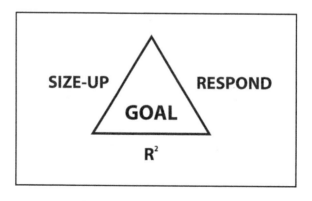

The Goal Assurance System is intended to be very flexible, and it is able to provide individuals, teams, and entire organizations a simple thought process that provides higher levels of goal achievement.

 **Hot Tip**

The Goal Assurance System is a cultural improvement because, in addition to other benefits, it also helps to prevent misunderstandings and communication breakdowns.

## Your Personal Goal Assurance System

On an individual basis, you can use GAS to think through tasks that are personal goals. Instead of the word "goal" in the triangle, actually visualize your particular goal. For example, if my goal is to leave for work by 7:00 a.m., I will visualize walking out my front door by 7:00 a.m.

Completing my size-up will allow me to quickly decide what I need to do to be able to leave by the prescribed time. I will plan for the appropriate time to take a shower, to get dressed, to eat breakfast, to check road conditions on my smartphone, and to add up how much time I need to be on my way by 7:00 a.m.—just as planned.

I will complete a brief $R^2$, and if I achieved my goal, I will mentally log it as a success. If, for example, my alarm didn't work, I would revise any future actions involving the alarm. I would make a note to self: Charge the battery.

Once on my way to work, I could have another goal: drive safely, for example. This allows me to do a quick size-up to remind myself how to accomplish a safe drive to work by considering weather conditions, traffic, buckling my seat belt, not texting, and so on.

When I arrive at work, I can set more goals. GAS is ideal for thinking on your feet as you go through your daily routine. This Goal Assurance System allows anyone to be productive and to effectively achieve success through goal attainment. Visualizing the GAS triangle will keep you focused on the goal—whatever you visualize it to be—and how to achieve it.

## Goal Assurance for All

Individuals, teams, companies, and organizations can benefit from the Goal Assurance System, because it is a tool that anyone and everyone can use to set and to achieve goals. Some of the components found in GAS are the same that are found in the formula for strategic thought process and success CPR + R². GAS can also be used as a strategic tool but is uniquely designed for tactical goal setting for individuals on the go. Because some of the principle components are shared between these two systems, the benefits and outcomes can be the same. It is important to note that the formula CPR + R² = Success is more robust and far reaching than GAS. This is because of how the success formula affects strategic problem solving, planning, and culture.

Managers, supervisors, and people at every level of leadership within an organization can also use GAS to gather the necessary information from their staff to make good decisions. As a team leader, when one of your team members comes to you asking for your approval for an initiative or project, you can use GAS to help guide your questions to get the information you need. Simply asking, "What is the goal?" is a powerful way to cut to the core issue.

You can also follow up with questions from the SIZE-UP Planning Process. Depending on your particular industry or profession, the SIZE-UP can be a great way to ask the right questions so that you have the information necessary for decision making. Once your decision is reached, your team can respond as planned.

Remember, you aren't finished until you have reviewed the outcome of the response, and during this review, you must decide if your goal has been reached. If so, then good for you, and you and your team can move on to the next goal.

You may still want to make revisions to your established procedures for future similar situations based on how the goal was attained. The successful actions that took place but weren't planned can be accentuated, evaluated, and debated for inclusion into current SOPs. The newly found revision becomes another addition to your best practices portfolio.

Most certainly, you will also want to make revisions to any failed processes or procedures to correct the failure. This is the process for turning failures into future successes. This is accomplished by utilizing the facts discovered during the review and then using the revise process to develop a plan to improve future outcomes.

GAS can be used to set goals at the highest levels of an organization. Boards of directors, CEOs, and every other leadership position can use GAS to get the organization on the road to goal assurance. When every individual in the organization is using GAS, the benefits are measurable. As business has moved from being relatively stable and uncomplicated to increasingly dynamic and complex, it is necessary to have tools that will allow everyone within your organization to maintain a focus on his or her goals. The difficulties of maintaining our focus while on the run and while sifting through all of the noise, distractions, and competing priorities can be eliminated with the Goal Assurance System.

While working in business, I discovered a situation that needed to be addressed to assist my teams in safely and effectively performing their duties. When receiving a flight request, it had become more and more difficult for my associates to sift through the complexities of the Federal Aviation Administration (FAA) regulations, safety procedures, state and county patient-care rules and regulations, and other restrictions—all making for a confusing process for the flight teams to rapidly assess.

During several review sessions of completed flights, I would hear a lot of confusion about what was the right thing to do in one situation or another. What I was hearing was the concerned voices of dedicated people who wanted to be the best that they could be. But due to competing rules and regulations, this motivation was becoming an obstacle to getting the work of the company accomplished. It was also becoming a possible safety issue.

I followed this thought process to help the flight crews define the goal for what they were being tasked with. By utilizing the Goal Assurance System, the crew receiving a medical flight knew that the initial goal was to answer the question, "Is it safe to accept the flight?" If the answer was no, they would decline or abort the flight request. If the answer was yes, they would move to the next goal by answering the question, "What is best for the patient?"

GAS allowed for simplifying an overly complex set of rules and regulations from aviation regulators, emergency medical oversight, and restrictions based on weather and other competing priorities and overlapping considerations.

## Did You Understand What I Think I Said?

Every individual involved with leading teams or giving instructions to others can use GAS to ensure their communications have been understood. Once you have communicated the information, start asking clarifying questions of your audience. Do this using the same process previously described, except that now you are asking questions to ensure that you were understood. For example, if I have just completed giving my team instructions for a particular task that they must accomplish, I will ask them, "What is the goal?" If there is hesitation or uncertainty coming from the team, I need to clarify the goal. I will follow by asking questions from my SIZE-UP and response plan. In this manner, I can be sure that my communications have been heard and understood.

In the fire service, this is one of the most critical elements of communications: knowing that others understand what is being communicated to them. In firefighting and in business, the better we communicate, the better the outcomes and the greater our successes will be.

 **Hot Tip**

Goal setting is a powerful process that allows you to find your focus and turns visualization into reality.

## The Fuel That Drives Future Successes

As a rookie firefighter in the Los Angeles fire academy, I found myself staring into that dark basement without GAS in my mental tool box. The fear and stress of that moment caused me to lose focus. Without a thought process like GAS, I was going nowhere, ready to succumb to all of the noise and distractions of the moment. I was ready to give up on my lifelong dream of becoming a firefighter. I had lost sight of my goal.

If the Goal Assurance System had been available, I would have had my goal in the front of my mind. I would have completed a SIZE-UP to identify the problems, obstacles, and challenges that were in my way and then developed a plan. Responding to that plan, I would have gone into the basement without all of the negative and self-destructive thoughts that had flooded my mind. I would have done what I had been trained to do with a bit more confidence. Later, I would have reviewed my actions and grown from the experience. I was lucky that I had leaders who identified early on that my body language was that of an unsettled mind, and an unsettled mind is helpless. Because the training captains quickly put me into the necessary situation, I was able to recover.

Every day, there are a countless number of people who fail to achieve— or even set—goals because they don't think that way. Even worse, these same people may not have leaders that create vision. It is so important to have leaders who clearly communicate their goals by stressing to everyone involved the role that he or she is to play a part in assuring that the stated goals are accomplished. Greg Vander Velde was the former director of product development for Alberto Culver, and this is what he thinks about Bird and his use of success principles like the Goal Assurance System:

> Jim brought strong leadership and innovation to the company. He distinguished himself as a key leader, delivered to the overall growth of the company, year over year, by consistently exceeding goals set for him.

As we review the successes that we have experienced, we can truthfully say that almost everything that has gone right in our lives can be credited to knowing what the goal was at the outset. The successes that we have enjoyed without knowing the goal first really came down to hit-or-miss circumstances or just dumb luck. Even when the goal was assigned to us by someone else, we had the habit of making it our own. To the contrary, we saw others with the habit of not setting goals, a behavior that was obviously not a recipe for assured success.

Goal setting is a powerful process that turns visualization into reality. It doesn't matter what the goal is or whether it is big and complex or small and simple. GAS can be the fuel that drives and delivers your future successes.

## Chapter Review: Empower Your People

The Goal Assurance System works to maintain your focus on your goals. Here is a review of how it provides everything you need to assure that your goals will be achieved:

1. What Is the Goal?: When deciding to do anything, the first step should be to ask, "What is the goal?" Remember, those who don't achieve goals don't set goals.
2. Finding Your Focus: Every work situation comes with the noise, distractions, and competing priorities that can cause you to lose focus on what you are trying to accomplish. Find and maintain your focus by visualizing your goal.
3. A Mind's-Eye View: The Goal Assurance System triangle is designed to be a mental picture that allows you to visualize your goal and the necessary steps you must take to accomplish it.
4. Individual Goal Assurance: GAS is ideal for thinking on your feet as you go about your daily routine. It allows you to be productive with the visualization that this process provides and the subconscious power that comes from maintaining a focus on your goal.
5. Team and Organizational Goal Assurance: GAS is also an excellent method for teams and entire organizations to employ when working on shared goals.

6. Improved Communications: GAS is a tool that will ensure communications have been heard and understood.
7. Fuel That Drives Future Success: Once you have formed the habit of setting goals and finding your focus to achieve those goals, opportunities will become your future successes.

## Revise: This Is Your Call to Action

1. What will you do differently in your work and in your life?
2. What is the size and scope of how you propose to improve?

## Part Three

# Transform Your Culture

In part 1, we covered process improvement principles. In part 2, we explored principles that are aimed at empowering your leadership and your workforce. And in part 3, we will illustrate how leadership's efforts to improve processes and empower people will ultimately cause a transformation of organizational culture.

By solving organizational problems that deal with process and people, leaders are making an improvement to the culture as well. The culture of the fire service is what we believe has been a major factor that allows for the continuous incremental improvement to process and for empowerment through personal development for people. When this occurs in any organization, there exists the right environment for a cultural transformation into what we refer to as the Class 1 Culture.

- In chapter 7, we share some simple improvements that will enhance management success and organizational thinking.
- In chapter 8, we provide a fictional tale of what a Class 1 Corporate Culture and inspirational leadership might look like in any organization.
- In chapter 9, we conclude with thoughts on how you can bring these fire-tested and business-proven principles of leadership and culture to life in your organization.

# 7

# The Two Most Important Questions for Project Managers

*The middle of every successful project looks like a disaster.*

—Rosabeth Moss Kanter

I walked into the front office one morning and asked my captain, "How's everything going this morning?" The captain jumped to his feet, ran over to the window, and looked outside.

After a brief pause, while still gazing outside, he replied, "I don't see any smoke, so everything is going just fine!" As I chuckled at his facetious response to my morning greeting, in a more serious tone, he went on to explain, "One of the great things about firefighting is that everyone knows how well you're doing your job if the city isn't burning. Another great thing is that every fire, no matter how big, eventually goes out. Our job is to make sure they go out sooner rather than later."

If the process of extinguishing destructive fires can be seen as analogous to successfully completing a business project, then collectively, the fire service has a 100 percent project-management completion success record. Of course, the outcomes are varied, but the cultural spirit in which firefighters take on the project of firefighting is commendable. No matter how difficult the situation becomes, they remain engaged until the project is completed. We believe that this same cultural spirit can be replicated in any organization. What would 100 percent project-management completion look like in your world?

The inspiration for this notion came to me one day in my post–fire service years, while working in business. I was sitting through a lifeless meeting on business project management and found myself reflecting on how differently the fire service takes on projects. The discussion at this project meeting was jumping from one subject to another and then back again. The only group dynamic was that of quiet chaos, as we were all making eye contact with each other along with facial expressions that reflected our confusion.

I think we were all wondering what the destination was for this project and the goal of this specific meeting was. There was no focus on a particular subject; no goals had been identified for the meeting; no situational awareness was evident; and all I could think was, *Why are we here?* To make matters worse, there was no discussion of resources available to tackle problems, no mention of resources already engaged in problem solving, and no progress report.

This rudderless meeting of upper and midlevel managers seemed to be going nowhere. By not communicating his vision for the project or even his goals for bringing everyone together, the individual conducting the meeting showed zero energy and had failed to take command. The leader of this meeting had not only failed to lead an agenda, he was also demonstrating zero enthusiasm for the subject matter. If our leaders aren't enthusiastic, why should anyone else be enthusiastic?

If this sounds familiar, whether you are the one leading the meeting or one of the uninspired participants, the fire service may have a better way.

## Two Questions That Must Be Answered First

Firefighters serve a mission that demands the use of management systems that work. These same systems that ensure firefighting success will allow any person, team, or project manager to respond successfully to everything from daily challenges to major projects.

As you know, firefighters respond to fires and other emergencies every day. Some of these fires are small and are extinguished with a single hoseline or fire extinguisher. Some are conflagrations, requiring a great deal of resources to extinguish. Yet, just as my captain pointed out, they are all eventually extinguished—project completed. That is a 100 percent effectual success rate for completing the project of firefighting. Business project managers can also employ some of the same principles and processes that fire service leaders utilize to achieve greater success. You can apply the same principles, but you will apply them from your perspective. Let's examine how a few simple improvements can make a huge difference in your project management success.

Sometimes the simplest things can seem so difficult to figure out when we are confronted with huge challenges all at once. Just imagine rolling up on the scene of a major fire with countless lives being threatened. You might be feeling overwhelmed and challenged by the information overload of the moment, trying to decide what should be accomplished first, second, and so on. Most people have probably been in similar situations, not really knowing where to start but wishing that they did.

Whether the challenge is a business project, a multifaceted program, or an aspect of change management or firefighting management, we really can't start making decisions regarding how to proceed with defining success or setting and prioritizing goals until we know the answers to the two most important questions:

1. What is the situation?
2. What resources are available?

To start and successfully complete a project, most business project managers will typically employ these same key stages, or something similar: initiation, planning, execution, maintenance and controlling, and closing. Still others will utilize very sophisticated systems with steps like: task, split, milestone, manual task, inactive summary, duration only, manual summary rollup, and so on. All of these steps are necessary for complicated and multidiscipline projects, to be sure. But even with very robust project-management procedures, there are a few potential improvements to leadership and culture that could make a big difference. This chapter is not a how-to on project management. The topic is complex and can be very specific and unique to the industry involved. The profession of project management can be technical in nature, but as with most technical professions, influential leadership can make a big difference in how things get done. With the right leadership, there can be some very important cultural improvements aimed at enhancing whatever process is used.

---

### 🔥 Hot Tip

The success of a business project is largely dependent upon the leadership abilities of the project manager.

---

Fires and other emergencies are chaotic and can be very large in size and complex in scope. Successful management relies on the collective efforts of all involved to effectively bring such a project to a close. To engage such a challenge requires a plan that includes specific strategies and tactics pertinent to the situation. Before a plan can be developed, a thorough knowledge of the situation and the resources that are available and can be deployed must be considered.

To lead a team effort takes enthusiastic leadership to inspire others to follow. Just as we described earlier in defining the success formula CPR + $R^2$, incident commanders must possess some critical abilities, to include critical thinking, strategic planning, and the right culture necessary to bring the project of firefighting and rescue to a successful close.

The success of a business project is also largely dependent on the leadership abilities of the project manager. Project managers must lead by taking advantage of every available system and tool to define problems, obstacles, and challenges (POCs) in order to identify resource needs. This process starts, however, by taking command of the situation. It includes identifying the current situation and identifying the resources available for utilization. The other steps involved in taking command of everything you do—to include managing your project—also apply: maintain two-way communications, define success, set and prioritize goals, and establish accountability.

## It All Starts by Taking Command

As a battalion chief responding with a full-alarm assignment to a reported structure fire, I was fully aware that I was in command of dozens of firefighters and millions of dollars' worth of firefighting apparatus and equipment, all rapidly converging onto the scene of the reported emergency. The situation that we would discover would be the focus of our collective future actions.

The first thing I would need to know was if the situation was static or dynamic. A static situation is defined as something that would not become any worse than when we arrived. An example of this is an unoccupied car, parked in the middle of a large empty parking lot, fully involved with fire. The damage has already been done to the car, and no amount of effort is going to change that. Additionally, with the vehicle being parked away from any other people or property, this fire cannot spread to do harm to any exposures. Time would be on our side.

The opposite encounter would be a dynamic situation. This situation is just like it sounds: things are actively happening. The more time it takes to get to work on solving the problem, the more damage will occur. An example of this would be a car that is fully involved with fire, but instead of being in the middle of an empty parking lot, this car has crashed into an occupied house, and flames are spreading into the structure. Time would not be on our side in this type of fire.

As in any dynamic situation, if there's also a report of people trapped inside the vehicle, the house, or both, then this second situation would demand a rapid response that would be capable of addressing the most critical problems in priority order. For this scenario, the first priority would be to save the most lives.

Keep in mind that as firefighting decisions go, so too go business decisions—but from a different perspective, of course. Get into the habit of asking yourself, *Is the situation static or dynamic?* And don't be afraid to consider what might happen if you do nothing. Sometimes, the less you do, the better the outcome. It all depends on the situation, the resources, and your ability to take command of both.

As my staff assistant drove our command vehicle into the parking lot of the large shopping mall where the fire was reported, I radioed the message, "Battalion 14 on scene and in command." The first on-scene engine captain had reported that there was nothing showing prior to my arrival. I knew the resources that were available to handle whatever challenges we might find, but I was still in the process of answering the first question: What is the situation? I was also looking to discover whether the situation was static or dynamic. This project of firefighting could not be planned until I could answer these critical questions.

Firefighters were beginning to check the stores for any sign of smoke or fire. Looking through windows, they discovered that most of the stores had already closed for the day. With night now upon us and visibility difficult, my staff assistant drove our command vehicle slowly to the rear of the 500-foot-long building. As we made our way, we were focused on looking for any sign of fire or smoke.

Additional resources began to arrive and report themselves on scene: "Engine 86 holding at Third and Main." I replied, "Roger, Engine 86—holding at Third and Main." This would repeat until all fire companies and rescue ambulances attached to this first-alarm assignment had arrived and were standing by for further direction.

## The Situation

Each project that you are assigned comes with its very own situation. Is it a static situation or a dynamic situation? Either way, we aren't looking to turn you into a firefighting leader; we just want to get you to start thinking a bit more like one. When you take on a new project, try to follow the same steps that a fire chief takes as the incident commander with the assigned project of firefighting.

We spotted some light smoke coming from a vent located on the roof and in the rear of the one-story mall. The address of the store was painted on the back door. I transmitted by radio to the first on-scene engine company to make entry and to assume the position of fire-attack in the involved unit.

We quickly returned to the front of the building in order to set up our command post (CP). Whenever possible, getting a quick view of all four sides of the building is considered a plus (while also considering all six sides of the emergency as described in the SIZE-UP Planning Process). Most fire chiefs will try to get a look at all four sides prior to selecting a spot to locate their command post, hopefully in a position that has the most advantageous view of the entire building.

Generally, the IC doesn't need to see the building that is involved with fire as long as he or she has excellent communication with the captains in command of the various teams working throughout the operational area. This is acceptable to me, but I also prefer to have a vantage point that enables me see the big picture. An optimum CP location allows the IC to read the smoke and flames, an action that assists in developing the strategy and tactics for attacking the fire. It also allows for real-time observation and analysis of the firefighting effort.

Try to imagine that you have been tasked with leading a project team to develop a new product that will provide a better way to do something. The problem is that you aren't allowed to ever see any drawings or prototypes of the new product, and you have no idea of how it should function. This situation would prove difficult to make decisions as you work to improve what is working and to troubleshoot what isn't.

In much the same way, there are times in firefighting where getting a visual is not going to be possible. When this happens, fire commanders rely on two-way communications as they use the SIZE-UP Planning Process. As you recall from previous chapters, this allows the IC to receive a 360-degree view of everything from their trusted eyes (firefighting team leaders: lieutenants, captains, chief officers) as the IC considers all six sides of the emergency. Still, nothing beats seeing the big picture with your own eyes whenever possible. But when it's not possible, seeing the situation and understanding the size and scope of the emergency through the eyes of a trusted team member can be just as effective.

As the first firefighters made their way into the involved store, their captain radioed that they had encountered heavy fire involvement in the rear and that the fire had also spread into the attic. I ordered an additional engine company from the nearby staging location to assist with fire attack. I also assigned two other engine companies to check on the exposures; one engine crew went into each store on either side of the store involved with fire.

In addition, I directed three truck companies to the roof to perform ventilation. Ventilation is an extensive subject as to the why and how of it. The benefits of ventilation operations are numerous, ranging from saving lives to protecting a greater amount of threatened property. The truck companies are specially equipped to perform this operation, which must be carefully coordinated with the engine company firefighters working hoselines inside the building. The truck company firefighters are trained to conduct ventilation procedures, very important and very dangerous tasks that involve working over the fire.

In this case, these firefighters vented the heat and smoke from the building by cutting, with chain saws and axes, heat holes through the roof directly over the fire. In addition to clearing much of the extreme heat and smoke from the building, this potentially hazardous ventilation operation will also prevent, for a short period of time, the fire from spreading horizontally. This is accomplished by channeling the heat vertically out through the heat holes, much like a chimney vents the heat and smoke from a fireplace.

This coordinated operation was made possible through face-to-face and radio communications between the IC, the engine company captains, and the truck company captains. The results of this well-coordinated project permitted the engine company firefighters, who were advancing hoselines inside the structure, to encounter less heat and smoke. The improved environment inside the building allowed the fire-attack teams to reach the seat of the fire more rapidly, reducing the fire's spread and halting its further destructive course.

 **Hot Tip**

By first knowing the current situation and the resources available, problems can be solved, obstacles overcome, and challenges successfully met.

## The Resources

Much like what happens when you take on a business project and you need to define the current situation, you must also identify the resources that are available for use in completing your project. The plan for the project assigned will not work well if the situation and the resources available—people, things, budgets, and time—don't fit your expectations. Whichever project management process you follow, knowing how your environment works operationally will go a long way toward delivering the best possible outcomes.

Initially, this fire was growing rapidly and had the potential to extend from store to store, destroying the entire 500-foot-long structure and everything in it. This project would require a rapid, coordinated attack strategy to achieve the priority-one goal of stopping the fire's spread.

As the fire-attack and ventilation teams went to work, I planned ahead by requesting additional resources from the dispatch center. I requested additional truck and engine companies, battalion chiefs, and rescue ambulances. I anticipated that each of the firefighters on scene would be using two to three air cylinders before achieving a knockdown on this fire, so I ordered a specialty team known as the emergency air unit to refill the firefighters' spent SCBA air cylinders. Additional command teams—battalion chiefs and their firefighter assistants—were ordered to create divisions of operations in order to keep the span of control at a safe and effective level. I now had enough resources, either on scene or en route, to equal a third-alarm fire.

This situation was similar to a business encountering grave economic or operational difficulties, both capable of causing the demise of any business. By first knowing the current situation and the resources available, problems can be solved; obstacles, overcome; and challenges, met. Any business can again become successful with well-defined plans, the right resources, teamwork, and innovative management and leadership principles.

All of the resources that I have mentioned here are from the LAFD. Most metropolitan fire department's core competencies come from within its organizational structure. However, there are times when firefighters will call on the core competencies of other departments, or authorities, to handle certain aspects of their work.

For instance, for emergencies involving hazardous materials, the fire department might handle the grunt work of identifying the hazard and mitigating most spills. Once the situation is contained and becomes static, a chemist from the appropriate authority would be called in to ensure the material is handled properly. There are situations where the fire department would also call for the assistance of a privately operated and licensed company that possesses the core competency to handle hazardous materials cleanup and disposal. The private professionals would then safely remove and transport the materials to the appropriate dumping facility.

Another example of calling for outside assistance is when firefighters run into a situation with an immediate need that is outside of their normal duties, not part of their core competency. For example, when the fire department answers a medical rescue call and firefighters are confronted with a violent person or someone with a weapon, they will always call for police support. The call, "Fire department needs help!" broadcasting over the radio waves would summon immediate assistance from law enforcement resources and additional fire command resources.

While working as part of a joint command with other agencies to bring a successful close to the entire incident, fire service commanders will always maintain command and control of their own resources. This is so leaders can ensure that any resource (human or otherwise) is only used in a manner that fits the resource's core competencies.

The main point here is to always build the core competencies of your teams. However, always use the core competencies of others for the specialty fields in which you do not have expertise or do not fully know how to handle the given situation. This gets to the critical need of recognizing the situation and understanding the resources that you have and the resources or competencies that you don't have.

## Documenting Your Way to Success

Project managers know how important documentation is to their process. It is also important to know why the documentation is being collected. Take the time to identify what information will be the most critical in maintaining situational and resource awareness to keep your project on track. And then match your documentation process to the same checklist that will not only measure progress but also identify problems as early as possible.

While I was ordering resources from the dispatch center, establishing a staging area, and assigning fire companies to different tasks or areas of responsibility, my staff assistant was busy writing down all of this information. He was recording everything on the situation status and resource status forms, a component known as the "Sit-Stat and Re-Stat System" for the incident action plan. This included the positions that each resource was assigned, the times for each assigned order, and the times of each update from the various resources.

In order to make decisions and to set priority goals for the incident, the IC must maintain constant situational awareness. The same is true for project managers. Using Sit-Stat and Re-Stat provides an up-to-the-minute dynamic history of the entire emergency incident. This is how situational awareness is maintained throughout the project of firefighting.

The IC must be able to continuously understand the status of all available resources and the situations in which each resource is engaged. This situational awareness is reflected in the IC's vision for how to successfully complete this project of firefighting and rescue. Situational awareness provides the information necessary to develop a strategic vision, create a plan, and maintain control of the plan while tracking each resource throughout the operational process. The outcome will be the realization of the shared vision: the successful conclusion of the emergency.

The Sit-Stat and Re-Stat System allowed me to set goals and assign tasks for each resource to accomplish. With my plan in place, these firefighting teams would be able to serve the greater vision by accomplishing each of the assigned goals, all contributing to stopping the fire's spread and finally achieving a knockdown.

As the situation changed, I continuously received information that was accurately and concisely collected through the use of two-way communication and PPN reporting. As this information came in, it was recorded to reflect changes. Once again, it is continuous situational awareness that is often a major factor in the project management of firefighting and rescue operations. Any conditions or activities reported were quickly analyzed to reveal their possible effects on the current and future planned actions. The actions of all the resources were tracked, documented, and confirmed. The leadership for the emergency operations was able to maintain this efficient status-keeping system by indicating positions, times, progress, and the needs for each. This also included the status of supervisory personnel. Whatever the situation requires, the appropriate resources are assigned to manage and control the challenges encountered.

For every complex emergency incident, the Sit-Stat and Re-Stat System is utilized to enhance constant situational awareness. From the beginning all the way through to the completion of the incident, all relevant information is consistently and accurately tracked and recorded with the Sit-Stat and Re-Stat System.

## Position, Progress, and Needs

Much like a project manager, for the incident commander, a critical element for success is to constantly monitor how all the participants are progressing and to be able to recognize trouble before it is too late to make the easy adjustments. To that end, another important motive for using Sit-Stat and Re-Stat is the ease of locating information for dissemination between leaders and any individual or group involved with the ongoing effort.

During firefighting operations, the IC or section commander maintains situational awareness through frequent two-way communication with all of the engaged resources. In previous chapters, we have explained the advantages of utilizing the communication component PPN in order to promote language of consistent two-way communication. This can also be beneficial for daily routine communications.

During firefighting, especially during complex and multifaceted operations, progress reports must be updated frequently. The fact that actions and changing conditions are occurring simultaneously requires a method to quickly and accurately exchange information. The enormous amount of messages transmitted during these emergencies necessitates that each message is transmitted as concisely and to the point as possible.

Your organization can use this process for communication and situational awareness improvement: PPN equals Position, Progress, and Needs. Think about your typical busy daily routine of meetings, phone calls, e-mails, and much more. Imagine running a conference call for a status meeting or a developmental update of a major prolonged initiative. From each reporting associate, you request, "Please report your PPN." This reporting process allows for a quick review to identify the areas where things are going well and where problems exist that you can now assist in resolving.

Knowing where the problem areas are as they occur speeds the execution of your corrective measures. By updating your ongoing situational awareness, you can take corrective measures that can keep a project on track, on time, and on or under budget. Visualize being able to quickly analyze the PPN information, update your situational awareness, and provide corrective measures. You are now leading from the front.

When a firefighter or team of firefighters gets into trouble and transmits an emergency call for help, immediate corrective measures can be lifesaving. However, the urgent help call can definitely interrupt the progress of the overall emergency operation. Because the IC is able to stay informed of operational difficulties and provide ongoing proactive corrective measures, PPN information often prevents the need for that urgent call for help in the first place.

For your business project management, use the communication tool PPN. It doesn't matter the type of project that you are managing. Leading with this easy method of information gathering will only complement your diligent efforts to continuously maintain situational awareness. This can avert the urgent calls for help, allowing you to make necessary changes before it's too late to save the day. This will happen if you infuse into your organizational culture a built-in mechanism where people are free to ask for help. What better way to ensure that your project will be a success than by knowing, before it's too late, that someone or something needs to be rescued?

## Your Rapid Intervention Team to the Rescue

Thanks to the Sit-Stat and Re-Stat System, the IC is able to recognize the location and the conditions in which every resource is engaged during an emergency incident. During firefighting operations, a crisis can put firefighter's lives at risk. In the worst-case scenarios, if rescue measures are not enacted immediately, firefighters will die.

Firefighters can become so focused and physically exhausted as they work to complete their assigned tasks that altering their actions effectively is not productive. When a potentially deadly event occurs during firefighter operations, such as a firefighter falling through a roof and becoming trapped in the fire area, the stress levels increase; emotions can create confusion for the firefighters currently engaged with the primary emergency. Quickly forming a rescue effort with the engaged firefighters of the primary emergency is not practical or effective for this immediate lifesaving situation.

The many operational obstacles to forming a rescue team from the firefighters working within the primary incident plan are evident: the need to replenish air cylinders, the cumbersome access of rescue tools from staged apparatus, and the physical exhaustion of the on-scene firefighters.

We have explained the consistent benefits that come from utilizing the $R^2$ Process following every firefighting operation. This invaluable cultural improvement has, once again, rewarded the fire service with a principle that has had an impact on the safety of all firefighters. It is known as a Rapid Intervention Team (RIT), and when applied to your business, the cultural improvement will be dramatic.

The use of an RIT was developed by the fire service and has saved many firefighters since its implementation. The RIT is an assembled team of firefighters who are preassigned and standing at the ready to respond to rescue the rescuers if necessary. The team is prepped, properly trained, and ready to respond with rescue tools, medical supplies, extra air cylinders, and specialized extrication equipment.

The important point is that a specifically trained team of firefighters from the ranks of the organization is available, with a focus on situational awareness, and standing by to intervene if necessary. Every firefighter in the department trains to be prepared for those occasions when their fire company receives the assignment announcing, "You are the RIT." The definition of success for the team is clear—save lives. The vision for the team will be dictated by the circumstances and clarified by the RIT leader. The values are the same values that each member of the team is normally held accountable for. In this case, firefighters are expected to exemplify—no matter what the conditions are—a will-do attitude. This is the attitude needed to realize their definition of success: saving your brother or sister firefighter.

> ### 🔥 Hot Tip
>
> The primary benefits are found in how a Rapid Intervention Team changes your culture to embrace teamwork, work ethic, accountability, productivity, and the subsequent successes that come with improving these organizational necessities.

In business, there are specific requirements for every task, profession, and position. Individuals come together to contribute their efforts to produce a product or service. You are the expert in your given field or profession. We don't know your business, but we do understand there are times in every organization when people or processes need to be rescued from potential failure.

The word "rescue" implies the sooner something happens, the better. Utilizing the RIT approach can help. Here's an example of how it has worked in business. There was a Fortune 500 company that employed the RIT concept during a major renovation to their information technology system. The senior management elected to organize a team from the existing management personnel; members of this team would be available to handle any problems that might occur with this enormous worldwide initiative.

Consequently, the senior management's foresight proved beneficial. The changeover was problematic, causing challenges for the continuing operations of the everyday business. However, due to proactively recruiting personnel from each of the numerous departments from the several sections of the organization, a team was assembled that could concentrate on solving problems, assuring compatibilities, and effectively installing the new system.

In this situation, the RIT members were alleviated of the majority of their daily routine responsibilities, allowing them to concentrate on the transition. Some problems were enormous, creating issues with production, sales, distribution, finance, logistics, and the interface with the previous IT system. A war room of sorts was established to provide the RIT with an atmosphere of teamwork. Eventually, the members of the RIT solved all of the problems, while the primary management teams continued their routine functions of providing progressive results for the everyday business as the new system was successfully installed. All of the members returned to their primary duties with gratitude and admiration from their fellow management associates.

This example from the Fortune 500 world was a huge success. What would it take to implement an RIT in your organization? The actual look and function is up to you to decide. What's important is that there are people who know they are part of the RIT and that there is a process to quickly bring them to the rescue when necessary. This could be a team prepared to provide analytics for sales and marketing initiatives, support for mechanical or technical renovations to improve production efficiencies, and much, much more.

Establishing an RIT for your business can be greatly beneficial. This system can assist your company's growth or help you to become more innovative in your field. It can be a system for continuing business as usual while also investigating alternative avenues of diversity to expand your operations and your horizons.

The primary benefits are found in how a Rapid Intervention Team changes your culture to embrace teamwork, work ethics, accountability, productivity, and the subsequent successes that come with improving these organizational necessities. The best part is how simple this process is to implement.

First, leaders take the time to assign a project, for example, to an individual or a team. Second, they identify one or more individuals who are considered the best at what they do by virtue of their education, training, experience, and work accomplishments. These people become the Rapid Intervention Team, or RIT, and they know that they are the go-to people to share their expertise when requested. Additionally, the project team knows that they are expected to call on the RIT for help in keeping things moving along on schedule and on or under budget.

In this scenario, those making up the RIT are not expected to do the work of the project team but are expected to provide advice, input, and guidance when requested. When companies and organizations function this way, they ensure that problems are discovered while there is still time to make the corrections and to save the project.

I worked for a company that hired me, pointed to my office, and then let me figure everything else out on my own. Because I was practicing the fire-fighting principles described in this book, in this particular organization, I was able to successfully overcome such challenges without much training or assistance early on. How much productive time has been lost by new employees who have not had the benefit of a Rapid Intervention Team to help them with a little advice, input, or guidance?

When your organization begins to utilize an RIT by making it part of your culture, you are taking a step that will ensure more successful results. By quickly identifying problems—with the expectation that your people seek assistance from someone at the ready who will respond to their call for help—your project management outcomes will be improved.

## Putting It All Together

Because leaders provide the foundational mission statement, they must also provide systems and processes that empower their people to successfully serve the same. No matter what type of business you are engaged in, Sit-Stat and Re-Stat is a system that will give your project managers and their project teams the 100 percent project-completion record enjoyed by fire service leaders.

Clarity is one of the most important qualities for successfully leading a project team. Leaders do this by giving a sense of purpose by enthusiastically communicating the vision and the goals of the project. Sit-Stat and Re-Stat is the system you can use to create and record your vision for the project, just as the fire chief created and recorded the vision for the project of firefighting. This system allows the progress of each team and individual working on the project to be continuously monitored and analyzed. It identifies specific responsibilities and recognizes where assistance is needed as well as which teams and individuals are available for additional tasks. By monitoring their progress at all times, Sit-Stat and Re-Stat provides you with the ability to easily track a number of projects simultaneously. Due to the documentation requirements, this system also provides a record to assist in conducting your review-and-revise sessions for continuous improvements and to further develop organizational best practices.

Without vision, there is no destination, and your people would have difficulty in understanding how to serve the greater good. Sit-Stat and Re-Stat provides the source information to update your project's vision and a method to communicate that vision to your people at all levels of your organization. This also allows for monitoring progress throughout the project by using feedback from two-way communications, including the practice of reporting with the speed and accuracy of PPN.

Expecting and receiving feedback is the other half of communication—the listening half. This is a simple process that allows leaders to take care of those on their team who respond to their requests. This is accomplished by supporting them with the tools, training, encouragement, and clarity needed to accomplish the assigned tasks and to complete the goals. This is referred to by the $N$ in PPN. Leaders will have the opportunity to lead from the front when they determine what is needed for their team members to succeed and then do whatever it takes to fulfill those needs.

The Sit-Stat and Re-Stat System is most important in times of crisis. Quite often, an IC can anticipate problems through the analysis of the situation and the current actions of the assigned resources. To be able to recognize adversity before it occurs is a benefit that comes with utilizing this system. For example, during firefighting operations, separate fire-attack teams may encounter a situation with opposing hose streams, and this can be a dangerous scenario for firefighters. This is a situation when firefighting teams are assigned to opposite sides of a fire. Depending on several factors, this alignment could result in the teams pushing the heat of the fire down upon each other with their hose streams. Due to extraordinary production of steam in a confined area, this has resulted in life-threatening burn injuries to firefighters in the past.

By continually reviewing the Sit-Stat and Re-Stat information, with PPN reporting from the involved resources as the situation constantly evolves, the IC can quickly recognize this type of physical arrangement of resources. This provides him or her with the ability to take appropriate mitigating actions to correct the unsafe conditions and to avert tragic injuries.

Business project managers will also find that this uncomplicated system will help identify issues before they become larger problems. By knowing and documenting the ongoing situation with your project and maintaining information on resources, you can accomplish what leaders must accomplish: clearly communicating your vision by providing a word picture of the successful completion of your team's effort. Sometimes this involves a change of plans due to unforeseen circumstances like opposing forces.

Remember, any team effort is only as strong as its weakest parts. Always ensure there is an RIT to respond to rescue, as quickly as possible, any part of the project that needs help. In addition, to experience greater collective project-management success, these two most important questions must be answered initially and throughout the project:

1. What is the situation?
2. What resources are available?

My business meeting experience reminded me of a more effective method for leading a meeting, inspiring others to buy into a project and to eliminate wasted time. It also reminded me that some of the best management systems are the simplest systems. Nothing is more frustrating than trying to cope with chaos and complexity by using tools that are, themselves, sources of chaos and complexity.

So, whether you're planning for a meeting, managing a project, organizing your own workload, or fighting a business fire, create a system that fits your particular organizational needs. This will ultimately allow your managers to always monitor the situation status and the resource status of their projects. Then employ a system that lets your leaders stay on top of the ongoing progress by using PPN in your communications. And be prepared for any contingency with an RIT. These simple improvements will deliver 100 percent project management completion, with the leadership and cultural improvement that comes with it.

## Chapter Review: Transform Your Culture

Whether your challenge is a project, a lengthy program, or management change, you really can't start making decisions on how to proceed in defining success or setting and prioritizing goals until you take the following into consideration:

1. It All Starts by Taking Command: The first thing you must do when you take command of a project is to answer the two most important questions. Your first step is to know the situation and whether it is static or dynamic and what resources are available to respond to the situation.
2. Situational Awareness: Understanding the current situation will enable you to develop your vision, define what success looks like, and set and prioritize goals.
3. The Resources: Understanding the resources available to you and how quickly the resources will be able to go to work is extremely important information as you develop your strategies and tactics.

4. Documentation: The documentation of your actions and the actions of all involved is vital information in order for you to maintain accurate and diligent situational awareness.

5. Position, Progress, and Needs: PPN is part of the two way-communication method that allows you to quickly, accurately, and concisely obtain feedback from all engaged participants and to determine the status of each one.

6. Rapid Intervention Team: It is extremely important that you have people who understand they are part of the Rapid Intervention Team (RIT) and that there is a process to quickly bring them to the rescue when necessary.

Whether you're planning for a meeting, managing a project, organizing your own workload, or fighting a business fire, develop the habit of beginning by answering the two most important questions.

## Revise: This Is Your Call to Action

1. What will you do differently in your work and in your life?
2. What is the size and scope of how you propose to improve?

# 8

# Igniting a Class 1 Culture

*The secret of achievement is to hold a picture of a successful outcome in the mind.*

—Henry David Thoreau

You might be asking yourself, *what now?* You've read the book up to this point, and possibly you're all in for the Class 1 Culture. But even though you have followed along throughout the different chapters, you aren't sure how to apply what you have just read. Or maybe you know exactly what you will do to make needed changes in your organization, your profession, and possibly even your personal life. Then again, you might be having a hard time seeing the true relevance for your business. Perhaps you are asking yourself, *What benefit can firefighting principles really bring to my business world?*

As my former fire academy captain pointed out, the only stupid question is the one that doesn't get asked. So, all good questions with answers sprinkled throughout this book. But just as firefighting is serious business, so too is every business, and we wouldn't expect anyone involved in his or her profession to follow a system or process about which that person is not certain. This chapter will hopefully further provide a business perspective to the firefighting principles that you have just read about. We wholeheartedly believe that if you take the time to become unconsciously competent with these principles—by igniting a culture that embraces change as an opportunity to experience greater success—you will have reinvented your thinking and the thinking of everyone within your company or organization.

These management, leadership, and success principles work collectively to create the Class 1 Culture that we've defined as an organization that is dedicated to being the best that it can be. The following is a fictional tale of how this type of culture and leadership might come together to improve your organization.

**Hot Tip**

Principles like these show what it is to be a Class 1 Culture: mentor others, improve team performance through the development of each individual's job satisfaction, and provide a work environment that is built on honesty, mutual respect, and trust.

## Jessica's First Day on the Job

Jessica was feeling nervous as she drove into the parking lot of ACME Manufacturing and Sales Incorporated. She had been looking for work for over six months, and now that she was finally starting a new job, she was a bit hesitant. Feeling a lack of self-confidence about taking on her new position plus a little fearful about what was to come made her think back to other moments in her life where she had experienced the same emotions. Jessica reminded herself that each time she had faced a new experience, it was actually the fear of the unknown that required her to courageously face and, ultimately, conquer her fears. She decided that, at 34 years old, she had to be brave. She told herself that this was no big deal. After all, she had the skills. She was just feeling nervous about doing something new and meeting new people. Jessica pulled into a parking space, took a deep breath, and was on her way.

Walking into the massive lobby of the ACME Manufacturing and Sales headquarters definitely impressed her. Everything looked very nice and clean, and she thought that her new work location was a place that she could get used to.

She was greeted by the receptionist, who joyfully said, "Good morning! How can I help you today?"

Jessica immediately felt relief because of the receptionist's friendly welcome. She started to have a very positive reaction about her new company, and her nervousness was beginning to subside.

She enthusiastically announced, "My name is Jessica Jones, and I have a nine o'clock meeting with Mary Green in HR."

Within a few minutes, Mary Green arrived at the receptionist counter and welcomed Jessica. As they walked side by side down a long hallway, Mary explained to Jessica, "Mr. Michael Summers is our president and CEO, and he insists on welcoming every new hire. He requested that I bring you in early this morning to fit his busy schedule."

Mr. Summers's administrative assistant escorted both Mary and Jessica into the nicely decorated office. Mr. Summers walked over to welcome the two. "Good morning, Mary. It is nice to see you, as always, and you must be Jessica Jones!"

As they shook hands, Jessica replied, "Yes I am. I'm very pleased to meet you!"

Mary explained to Mr. Summers, "Jessica is the new assistant sales manager in the electronics division."

Mr. Summers sat in the chair behind his desk, and said to them both, "Please, sit down and make yourselves comfortable." As the meeting progressed, Mr. Summers shared some success stories from ACME history, and he also told a few stories about failures that, ultimately, turned into successes.

Jessica asked, "Mr. Summers, what is the most important advice you could give me to be successful. What does a successful assistant sales manager in the electronics division look like?"

Mr. Summers replied, "First of all, please call me Michael. Now, I'm glad you asked that question, because I do have a few things to tell you about our company and why we are so successful." He continued, "ACME Manufacturing and Sales Incorporated is all about our people. We manage our processes, but as a manager yourself, you are expected to lead your people. Our culture is all about what we do and why doing it well always matters to someone. What I mean is that each of our employees knows that their work here is important to our collective success. In fact, every position and everything we do is necessary. We also require all of our employees to put a face on who benefits when they do their job to the best of their abilities. Think about it: Who does it matter to?"

Jessica was all ears as she listened to Michael say things that she had never heard from anyone, including her former bosses. She was taking it all in as she noticed a small brass plaque on Michael's desk that read: "We're class 1, and it shows!" Expressing her immediate reaction, she said, "This is all such a unique way of thinking, especially in business, and I really like what I'm hearing." Pointing to the brass plaque, she asked, "What does 'We're class 1, and it shows' mean?"

Michael replied, "Oh, that . . . class 1 refers to the culture here at ACME. The definition is really what I just explained: Our people believe what they do is important, and doing it well always matters to someone. But it is really so much more, because as leaders in the company, we need to provide our people with the right culture that supports such a notion."

Jessica asked, "How do you accomplish that?"

Mary interjected, "Our next stop will be the HR office, and I will be able to answer more of your questions about expectations and how we operate . . . things like that."

Smiling, Michael quipped, "You don't know what you've gotten yourself into, Jessica! But before you go, I do want to share three things with you that are very important to our company's' success: our mission, vision, and values."

Michael sat forward in his chair, and looking very enthusiastic, he continued, "First, our mission statement is hanging in every office and meeting room in the building. It is important for you to know it and use it as a foundation for thought and action. It really defines ACME's core reason for existing. Every leader is accountable for ensuring that our mission statement is truly a driver for decision making. This is important because without a unifying mission, our people would be going in different directions and creating their own agendas; our mission is where our teamwork starts!"

Taking a slight pause so that Jessica could complete the notes she was jotting down, Michael took a sip of water from the water bottle on his desk. He continued, "The second is our vision statement, which is, where we are going as a company and what we are all striving to achieve collectively. Regardless of the department or division you call home or your job title, for that matter, every single employee needs to understand my vision for ACME and how he or she will personally contribute to making that vision a reality. This is also hanging in every room, right next to the mission statement, because without vision, there's no destination."

Again he paused briefly, letting Jessica finish what she was writing on her notepad. Pointing at the wall in front of his desk, Michael said, "And third, hanging alongside the first two, is our values. Everyone is expected to uphold these values, and everyone is also expected to hold each other accountable for these values. You know, without values to guide everyone's performance expectations, well, there would only be chaos!"

Jessica was feeling like she wasn't able to capture everything she wanted to in her notes. She thought, *This all sounds so meaningful, so good and useful, but it had been said, and now . . .* Jessica asked, "Michael, these are such wonderful insights, but I'm not sure I got it all down. Do you have something in writing?"

Smiling momentarily at Mary, Michael looked back at Jessica and replied, "Not to worry, Jessica, Mary will fill you in on these and many other principles that we live by, and you will get them in writing. Jessica, I really appreciate your taking the time to come in and meet with me, and I am very glad that you are part of our team. So, welcome to ACME, and best of luck with your new position. You have a great sales team, and I am counting on you to do your best!"

Jessica shook Michael's hand, thanking him for the opportunity to be part of the team, and then Mary and Jessica headed for the HR office.

Taking a seat at her desk, Mary said to Jessica, who was still standing, "Please take a seat and get comfortable, because we have a lot of things to cover."

Jessica sat down in a chair facing Mary and said, "I really like Michael. He seems so connected to all aspects of the company, and he made me feel at ease and appreciated."

Mary replied, nodding her head in agreement. "Michael is one of those leaders who lead by example. If you try to follow his lead, you won't go wrong!" Mary began to pull out routine paper work for Jessica to complete. She also pulled out an employee manual and handed it to Jessica.

Jessica took the manual and read familiar words, right there on the front cover: We're class 1, and it shows! "Why is this Class 1 Culture such a big deal?" she asked.

Mary replied, "It's a big deal because it really comes down to a way of thinking. This manual will explain how our culture works and how you, as a leader, will be accountable for ensuring that your team benefits from the principles that make such a culture possible."

Jessica couldn't help but think back to previous employers, coworkers, and supervisors. None of them ever discussed things like putting a face on who benefits when you do your best. She felt intrigued by everything she had seen and heard thus far.

"Mary, this might sound odd, but everywhere else that I have worked . . . well, most people wanted to know what was in it for them before they bought in to follow along with any work requirements. Do ACME employees buy in, not push back?"

Mary smiled and said, "Well, when your people see their work as a fulfillment of who they are, and they believe that it is in their best interest to do it well, they want to be more accountable and productive. With the right culture in place, doing one's best *is* what's in it for them." With that said, they were off to meet Jessica's immediate supervisor and her new team.

As they walked along, Mary explained to Jessica that the electronics division's sales team was conducting a meeting and that it would be a great time to meet everyone at once. Just thinking about walking into the conference room was making Jessica feel anxious and a bit stressed. She remembered her decision to be brave, and then she took a deep breath.

Mary swung open the conference room door. As Jessica walked into the room, looking at a large group of strangers, Mary announced, "Hello, everyone. I apologize for the interruption, but I wanted to introduce you to your new assistant sales manager while you are all in one place. Everyone, this is Jessica Jones. And, Jessica, this is your sales team, including your new boss, Bob Mason!"

Bob walked up to Jessica, welcomed her, and shook her hand. Everyone in the room greeted her with a friendly smile and a sincere, "Hello, nice to meet you," or "Welcome to the team!" Jessica was no longer feeling stressed or nervous; she was feeling excited about her new job and couldn't wait to get to work!

Bob pointed out that the team was just finishing up with their weekly review, and if Jessica had the time, he would like to sit down with her to bring her up to speed on her new position. Mary agreed that both Jessica and Bob should get started with an introductory meeting and that Jessica could come by HR at the end of the day to finish her orientation paperwork. Bob gathered up his belongings, and then he and Jessica headed for her new office.

Walking into the office of the assistant sales manager, Bob enthusiastically said, "Well, here it is, Jessica: your new home away from home!"

Stepping through the doorway, Jessica looked around the room. She saw that it was fairly plain, but she couldn't help noticing the mission, vision, and values that hung on the wall directly across from her desk. She could readily imagine that every time she looked up from her desk, she would be reminded of the ACME drivers of success. Then she saw the plaque on her desk.

Jessica said, "Bob, I really want to learn more about this class 1 thing. It seems to be such an important aspect to this company and how it functions, but I don't fully get it. It sounds great, but I'm not sure . . . I mean, how do I take advantage of it, I guess?"

Bob replied, "Jessica, you sound a bit confused, but not to worry. We all start off in much the same way. In answer to your question, when the members of your workforce believe what they do is important and that doing it well always matters to someone—when that happens, everyone will have the best opportunity to go from ordinary to extraordinary performance. This defines the Class 1 Culture."

Still feeling a bit confused, she asked, "Can you tell me exactly what I should be doing in order to be part of this Class 1 Culture?"

"Sure, let me explain it from your perspective as a leader in this company and, more specifically, as my assistant manager. Think about your leadership style. Whatever style you have developed to this point in your career, I need you to make sure it includes: mentoring others, improving your team's performance through developing each individual's job satisfaction, and always striving to provide a work environment that is built on honesty, mutual respect, and trust. When you focus on these principles, you are showing what it is to be class 1."

Jessica was feeling very excited, as she was beginning to understand this new business culture. With a smile on her face, she said, "Thank you. That makes so much sense. I can definitely do that! Does everyone, in every position actually do these things?"

"Yes, if they want to be part of our team, they do. It is an expectation of leadership."

Jessica was feeling really good about her new job and the business environment that she was now a part of. It all seemed so uplifting! She asked, "So, the Class 1 Culture is basically a leadership responsibility, and when we mentor, build trust, and respect people within our team, good things will happen, right?"

"Well, sort of, but there is so much more to it," Bob explained. "In fact, it will take you some time to learn all of the principles that make it all work."

Feeling eager to find more information, Jessica interrupted by asking, "How do I learn these things? Where is it written?"

Bob went on to explain, "Ultimately, the Class 1 Culture is about strategy, tactics, teamwork, and a positive attitude." He gave her examples from his tenure with ACME that demonstrated the need for everyone to strive for success 100 percent of the time. He told her, "All of the principles that you will be learning in the weeks to come are simply tools that allow all of us, not just the leaders—everyone, to continuously improve our performance, to be empowered and accountable problem solvers, and to continuously transform our culture to be the best. You know, we will all succeed, or fail, together. An example of this is the meeting that our sales team was just having. It was a review of our weekly activities. I always lead this meeting; in the future, you will also take your turn at leading it. The way it works is that we go around the room reporting, briefly, what has gone right and why, what has gone wrong and why, and what issues need to be discussed in a revise meeting."

Jessica asked, "You do this every week?"

"Yes, this is how each and every team functions at ACME. We are all expected to review everything we do in search of best practices. Even when things go well, we want to know why so that we can replicate the successes as a best practice. This review-and-revise process is known as $R^2$, but I don't want to go into all of the finer points right now. Just know this: When you apply this process to everything that you and your team complete, the results are dramatic—dramatically good!"

Jessica was satisfied by Bob's explanation but still not sure about how to make this all part of her thinking. Jessica said, "Well, this all sounds impressive, but I'm still not seeing exactly how I contribute effectively to this success-driven culture."

Bob understood Jessica's concerns. It had not been very long since Bob was in the same position, new to ACME and not really understanding this new way of thinking. Bob remembered what his mentor had taught him when he was first hired and shared it with Jessica. "Think of those times in your past work experience where people didn't take ownership for solving problems. They expected management to solve any problems, obstacles, or challenges that came their way. My experience with that type of business culture is that it always resulted in low accountability, poor customer service, confusing communications, zero motivation, decreased productivity, lack of teamwork, and an inferior work ethic. The principles that are part of ACME's culture prevent all of those negative outcomes from happening. Your employee manual explains the principles that are part of our Class 1 Culture, and I will help you to understand how to apply each and every one of them. Trust me, they are all common-sense tools and simple to apply, and best of all, they work!"

Jessica felt relieved that her new boss was so helpful and really seemed to care about her future success. Her first day at ACME Manufacturing and Sales turned out to be a pleasant surprise. Heading for home, she was walking through the lobby toward the exit, when she spotted the counter where the receptionist had greeted her that morning. Because it was past closing time, the receptionist was not at her post. Jessica wanted to thank her for the warm welcome she received that morning. She also wanted to properly introduce herself and to learn the receptionist's name. She figured that it would have to wait until tomorrow.

Turning around to leave, she noticed a small sign on the counter, facing the receptionist's chair. The sign read, "Will do!" Jessica thought, *Now, what does that mean?*

As she pondered the sign, her thoughts were interrupted by someone saying, "Jessica, you can't stay here all night. It's time to go home!" Jessica turned to look, and it was Michael Summers.

"Oh, hi, Michael. I was just trying to figure out what 'Will do' means."

"Well, it is part of our Class 1 Culture. Because everything we do is important and doing things right always matters to someone, we can't just believe in can-do; we must believe in 'will-do.'" As Michael walked toward the exit, he added, "It's our company motto. Have a good night. I'll see you in the morning!"

Jessica enthusiastically and cheerfully replied, "Will do!"

When Jessica got home, she couldn't wait to open her employee manual. She was eager to start reading about all of the new things she was now accountable for applying in her new position at work. She had about an hour before her fiancé, Doug, would pick her up for a dinner date.

As she read through the table of contents, she saw entries that read: Mission, Vision, Values, Command, Plan, Respond, You Go . . . I Go: Teamwork, Will-Do, Sit-Stat, Re-Stat, SIZE-UP, GAS, POC, PPN, RIT, SOP, and $R^2$. As she began to read about each of these topics, she was beginning to see how they all worked together to support what she had learned was the definition of a Class 1 Culture. These principles, she was beginning to realize, seemed fairly simple to use. Combined, they definitely seemed to provide a useful, practical, and flexible way to influence positive thinking and teamwork and to bring about successful outcomes. When she thought about it, she was beginning to realize that these principles really described what leadership is all about.

Doug arrived right on time, and as they drove to dinner, he asked, "So, what do you think about your new job?"

Jessica said, smiling widely, "I love it! Everyone is so nice. It is a very positive place to work, and they are all about mentoring and supporting their people and cultivating honesty, trust, and respect. I could go on and on."

Doug jumped in and said, "Wow, I can't remember the last time you were this excited about a job!"

Jessica thought for a moment and then said, "You know, I don't think I have ever been this excited about a job—but you have! Remember how you felt when you were first hired to become a firefighter and were going through the fire academy? Remember those feelings you had about your job that you would share with me?"

Doug thought about what Jessica had said, replying, "I do remember. In fact, those feelings never went away. They have only become more pronounced. So, what is it that makes this place so different than the other companies that you have worked for?"

"Well, for one, they have this thing they call a Class 1 Culture. In fact, on every desk, I saw a small plaque with the words, "We're class 1, and it shows.""

Listening intently, Doug looked at Jessica for so long that she blurted out, "Keep your eyes on the road, buddy!"

Looking back toward the windshield, he replied, "Oh, sorry about that . . . but, class 1? That's a fire department term."

"Are you sure?" Jessica asked.

Doug went on to explain to Jessica, "For a fire department to achieve a class 1 rating is a huge accomplishment because it reflects a firefighting organization that is dedicated to doing things right. Class 1 is the highest rating, and it means that they are the best at what they do!"

All through dinner, Jessica's thoughts kept coming back to what Doug had said about the fire department and what it meant to be class 1. She felt fortunate to have been hired by a company that believed in a culture that had the power to inspire success. For the first time in a very long time, Jessica was looking forward to going to work in the morning.

---

### 🔥 Hot Tip

A Class 1 Culture not only improves your organization but also ultimately enhances your brand by giving your leaders, your workforce, and your customers a good feeling about what you do and why you do it.

---

## Your New Beginning

We have experienced how a class 1 way of thinking will improve the performance of anyone involved in any type of business or organization. It has taken over 30 years to develop, test, and prove the management, leadership, and success principles that have been shared in this book. If you use these principles and processes in your daily routine to improve individual, team, and organizational performance, in a short period of time, you will also see the benefits in these key areas: accountability, best practices, customer service, communications, morale, motivation, productivity, teamwork, and work ethic.

It is important to remember that no one knows the vision you have for your organization better than you do. Because of that, this book is not a how-to. It is actually a "how you" can be more successful in sharing your vision and effectively transferring that vision to all of your leaders and employees. Lighting a fire under your business by igniting a Class 1 Culture not only improves your organization but also ultimately enhances your brand by giving your leaders, your workforce, and your customers a good feeling about what you do and why you do it.

The Class 1 Culture requires the cooperative thinking that everyone will succeed or fail together. The mission of this book is to inspire success by influencing individual, team, and organizational behavior. We have revealed proven methods that will start the process of self-examination into how you feel about what you do and why you do it.

Our vision is to change how people view their role in their work and in their life. After reading this book, we see people responding to their business challenges with a resolve that will make success their focus. Your teams, your entire organization, and even your friends will perform at a higher level when, intrinsically, there is a belief that what they do is important and they will be inspired to be at their best. This is because whatever they do, they will understand why giving their best performance always matters to someone.

Making the shift to a Class 1 Culture will not happen overnight. However, the transition can be enhanced by your leadership, as you demonstrate by example that this cultural improvement is a priority. With the principles described throughout this book, you can provide the motivation and inspiration for people to become the best that they can be. You now have the power to inspire everyone around you to perform in a way that demonstrates a new appreciation for what they do and why they do it.

## Chapter Review: Transform Your Culture

Take the time to read back through all of the chapter reviews. As you do, try to be mindful of the unique aspects of your organization and how best to apply these principles into your work environment. We have already adapted these principles of firefighting for use in any organization. Your situation may require additional adaptation. With the right perspective, you will be able to build a Class 1 corporate culture with your own inspirational leadership.

## Revise: This Is Your Call to Action

1. What will you do differently in your work and in your life?
2. What is the size and scope of how you propose to improve?

9

# Conclusion: The Spark That Ignites

*If your actions inspire others to dream more, learn more, do more and become more, you are a leader.*

—John Quincy Adams

My first firefighting encounter in that basement had a tremendous impact on the rest of my life. I didn't realize it at the time, but my life was being transformed. I was being prepared for future achievements—through continuous incremental improvements—that would shape who I was in a very positive way. These daily improvements would not only allow me to succeed at my firefighting career; they would also encourage me to try new things after my fire service career had ended. To paraphrase the chapter's opening quotation from John Quincy Adams, these successes were the result of being able to dream more, learn more, do more, and become more because I had been inspired by the culture, and the leadership found in the American fire service.

As we have previously pointed out, firefighting is a hot, dirty, and dangerous environment. And yet, it has also been a great place for us to discover real-world business principles that work. Big fires start small, just like a big accomplishment starts with a single idea. Best practices can spread faster than wildfire if they are shared with others. What will you do now that you have at your fingertips these management, leadership, and success principles that, together, represent the Class 1 Culture?

Once again, it all starts with how you respond and apply these principles that have the power to create success in whatever you are doing. How do you improve your process, empower your people, and transform your culture in a way that delivers what you are looking for? How will you light a fire under your business or organization, and what does it look like when you do?

We have shared numerous principles that have a successful track record in certain organizational situations. We have also created a fictional story to illustrate the potential for any organization willing to adopt and infuse these principles into its culture. Most likely, not all of these principles will be necessary or practical in some work environments. But whichever principles you choose to put into practice, you must remember to first ask yourself and your leadership team: "What specifically are we trying to improve upon, and what results are we looking for?" Keep in mind that in both firefighting and in business, preparation is the key, success must be the expectation, and continuous improvement is crucial for organizational survival and future dramatic results.

With these three points in mind, how do you change the thinking in your organization to reflect the value of preparation, successful expectations, and continuous incremental improvements? Will these changes improve your process, empower your people, and transform your culture? If you are going to choose a path forward, wouldn't it be beneficial to own a thought process that can take you to your desired destination?

To start with, put together mission, vision, and values statements such as those we have expounded upon. This single step will positively impact your process by putting the focus on what you think is important. It will also empower your people with the right thoughts and actions to succeed in your business environment.

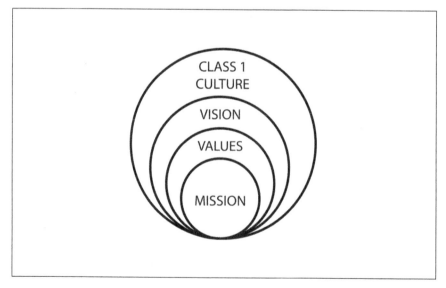

**FIGURE 9.1**

Even though we have listed these drivers of success as mission, vision, and values, they actually work in a different order. Refer to Figure 9.1; it represents how the mission statement provides your organization with a foundation, and the values are what your people will use to collectively bring the organization's vision to life. When these three elements are in place, along with inspirational leadership and other culturally transformative principles, the Class 1 Culture will be yours.

Your leaders will need to show the way if your culture is going to experience the transformation needed to experience the success you want, via daily improvements; think of a success formula. The role for leadership in this process has been explained and must be a central theme in your organization. Nothing lasting will ever occur within any organization if it isn't exemplified by every level of leadership, to include the top spot. What does it look like when anyone influences others and inspires them to think differently? Here's an example of what could happen.

In one of my former business positions as a regional director for a company in the air medical industry, I was tasked with setting up a thank-you lunch for the two loan officers who had put together a deal that made it possible for the company to purchase $25 million worth of helicopters. Their hard work and efforts allowed our company to replace much of its aging fleet. As a way to thank these two businessmen, my team planned on taking them out to a nice lunch, followed by a flight in one of our new helicopters. We did this at our base located in South Lake Tahoe, California. The lunch was pleasant, but our guests seemed a bit distant and out of place. They were friendly gentlemen, but our conversation never got beyond the superficial. Once we got back to the base, we went on a 20-minute flight around Lake Tahoe to show off some of the spectacular sights that our medical flight crews get to experience on a daily basis. The comments made by this banking duo were mainly about how beautiful the region is and not much more. When the flight was concluded, I walked these men back to their car.

As we stopped near the parking lot to say our good-byes, I said, "We all really appreciate everything that you two did to make this loan happen. In fact, what you did wasn't just moving millions of dollars around. Your efforts have provided our flight crews with safer, state-of-the-art aircraft. It also provided the communities we serve with more reliable helicopters, and every time these pilots and nurses successfully save a life, both of you own a piece of that because we couldn't do it without your help."

When the last word exited my mouth, I noticed a profound change in each man's demeanor. Now, with smiles on each of their faces, one of the gentlemen looked at the other and said, in a sincere tone, "Wow, who knew we were actually saving lives. I can't wait to tell my kids what I did today!"

When they turned to walk toward their car, they both seemed to be standing a bit taller. It doesn't matter who you are leading—a firefighting team, a business team, or a couple of account managers—it is your inspirational words that do matter. Once you have learned the value of helping others to understand that what they do is important and why doing it well always matters to someone, you have become an inspirational leader. When your leadership team does this routinely, your people will be empowered to focus on success. This is because each and every one of them will have a better idea of what success looks like to him or her. Most people will always work harder to accomplish the things that they think are important.

You have seen the following list of benefits before, and it is so important to your future successes that we will say it again. When you look at all of the principles and tools described in this book, you will have the ingredients that are necessary to bring about improvement in these very critical areas: accountability, discovering and implementing best practices, communications, customer service, morale, motivation, productivity, teamwork, and work ethic.

Take the time to know and understand your current organizational situation and how you want to improve it. Then take a second look at the principles and tools that we have provided throughout this book. You and your team, together, should decide which of these principles and tools will deliver precisely what you are looking for.

It only takes a spark of inspiration to make a huge difference when it comes to improving organizational culture and leadership. Ultimately, this can improve your process, empower your people, and transform your culture in a way that is right for you and your organization. Remember that success belongs to those who believe it's possible, who know how to define it, and who are motivated to create it. If this doesn't describe the current situation within your organization, then the business fire alarm has just sounded. It is time for you to respond as though it matters and begin building a Class 1 Corporate Culture.

# Index

## About the Authors

**TOM PANDOLA** spent more than two decades solving problems associated with fires, floods, riots, earthquakes, and more with the Los Angeles City Fire Department. His many leadership assignments included the commander of air operations and the hazardous materials task-force commander. After "retirement," he took the fire-tested principles that he learned on the front lines of firefighting with him to the business world. Working as a regional director in the high-stakes business of emergency air medical transportation, he improved operational effectiveness through teamwork, empowered the workforce with the confidence to make good decisions, and ultimately transformed the culture into one that was dedicated to be the best. Pandola is a partner of Third Alarm, a company he founded with his coauthor, Jim Bird. For the business professionals he consults with and coaches as well the audiences he speaks to, his mission is to inspire success with these fire-tested and business-proven principles of leadership and culture.

**JAMES W. BIRD** served for 24 years with the Los Angeles City Fire Department, rising to the rank of captain, where he distinguished himself as an innovative leader. In addition to leading his firefighting teams into and safely out of dangerous situations, he also worked diligently to make a difference in other key areas. For example, he designed, developed, and coordinated a highly successful fire-prevention and incident-reduction program involving both public agencies and private businesses. He also designed and developed a highly successful women's firefighter training program that was the first of its kind in the country. These are just a few of his fire service career accomplishments.

Bird took his firefighting principles of management, leadership, and success with him to excel in business. Hired by St. Ives Laboratories, Inc. (with annual sales over $100 million) to manage the obsolescence of finished goods, Bird eagerly took on the challenge. Tasked with reducing a $5 million to $8 million annual loss, he turned it into an annual gain of $2 million to $3 million over a five-year period. Using the same principles that brought him success during his fire service career, he took on a seemingly impossible task and invented, designed operations, and administered a new way to do business. The remarketing department was born. This example defines the terms "fire tested" and "business proven." Bird's business career spanned 20 years in the high-pressure environment of the Fortune 500 sector. In addition to St. Ives Laboratories, he also worked for Alberto Culver and Unilever as he developed new sales strategies and cross-functional processes while providing leadership for diverse teams. He achieved success in each of these businesses without any prior formal business education—only the adapted firefighting principles that he brought with him to guide his thinking and his actions.

Along with Tom Pandola, Bird is a founder and partner in the company Third Alarm. His insights and business experiences have been paramount in developing the principles that can improve individuals, teams, and entire organizations through inspirational leadership and culture.